AN ARIZONA CHRONOLOGY

THE TERRITORIAL YEARS
1846-1912

Douglas D. Martin

THE UNIVERSITY OF ARIZONA PRESS

TUCSON   1963

The University of Arizona Press
www.uapress.arizona.edu

Printed in the United States of America
21   20   19   18   17   16   7   6   5   4   3   2

ISBN-13: 978-0-8165-0005-5 (paper)
ISBN-13: 978-0-8165-3533-0 (Century Collection paper)

The eighty pages of type for *An Arizona Chronology* were set in Times
Roman by Morneau Typographers.

L. C. No. 63-11975

♾ This paper meets the requirements of ANSI/NISO Z39.48-1992
(Permanence of Paper).

Errata

1853	Dec. 30	The second line should read "45,535 square miles."
1871	April 10	The date was April 30
1887	Sept. 29	The year was 1877
1890	Feb. 15	The year was 1900
1890	July 16	The year was 1900

FOREWORD

When Douglas D. Martin first brought the idea for *An Arizona Chronology* to the editors of the University Press, we were dubious about the project. As the work progressed, however, our fascination grew, and with the completion of the first volume, "The Territorial Years," we began to realize that what Martin has done is unique. Rarely does a chronology capture so fully the record or the flavor of a period. Martin has done for the Territorial period almost what he did for *Tombstone's Epitaph*. And while the first volume closes with statehood, he is busy at work with two other volumes which the University Press will publish upon completion.

Originally Martin intended to compile his chronology exclusively from the newspapers of the period. He found, however, that too much would be left out, and he expanded his sources to include other basic historical materials.

The result is a fascinating reference book which vividly recalls Territorial days, while pointing to important sources from which the reader may amplify his interest. Critics of this volume may argue that it is incomplete, since such and such a "fact" has been left out. Such omissions are inevitably true of chronologies, but consider what Martin has added: the selectivity of an experienced, and wise editor whose newspaper career includes *two* Pulitzer prizes. *An Arizona Chronology* viewed through Doug Martin's eyes must necessarily take on an excitement of its own.

It is our belief that it has.

THE EDITORS

INTRODUCTION

Arizona has been the subject of several general histories and a number of volumes treating special subjects peripherally related to history. This book, however, is somewhat of a new venture in recording the state, a chronology rather than a narrative, not simply recording events of importance and interest in Territorial Arizona, but pinpointing them in time.

The chronology will not replace older histories but may serve as a new and ready source of information, helpful to researchers, writers, teachers, and students, and of interest as well to the general reader.

One thousand facts and dates are gathered here from the period ushered in by the war with Mexico and ended by statehood. Of course not every important fact was gathered, and readers may well know of events and items which would equally warrant inclusion. This could not be avoided, for there are gaps in existing reference material caused by the fact that many dates were never recorded, or if recorded, were later lost.

Neither custodians nor historians should be criticized for this. They have done wonderfully well, despite discouragement caused by flood, fire, death, and most of all the understandable failure of an unself-conscious people, involved in a consuming struggle for self-preservation, to place great importance on saving records of their daily lives.

It would have been comparatively simple to gather and date most of the outstanding events in Territorial history, and to stop there. But had this been done, we would have only the skeleton — the cold letter of the past. We would miss the human touch, the short steps by which people went forward, and the spirit in which they strained for every measure of advance. "The letter killeth, but the spirit giveth life."

That the larger task was possible is due to the daily and weekly press of Arizona, born four years before this became a Territory, boasting a record of service interrupted only when General Carleton's men wrecked the one handpress in the Southwest in a crude attempt to produce a Union paper.

Newspapers and Periodicals of Arizona, "University of Arizona Bulletin No. 15," compiled by Miss Estelle Luttrell in 1950, shows that between March 3, 1859 when *The Weekly Arizonian* first appeared at Tubac, and statehood in 1912, a total of 155 weekly and daily newspapers appeared. If Spanish-language papers and publications concerned with mining, cattle, agriculture, labor, and education were included, the number would be even larger.

The mortality rate of Territorial newspapers was high. The smallest towns sometimes boasted a printer with a few fonts of type, and a can of ink. Many such papers and the towns where they were born died early, like La Paz on the Colorado River. Some of the towns were buried by time, others are ghost towns or less: Peach Springs, Harshaw, Quijotoa.

Little newspapers in mining towns usually folded when the ore vanished. Change in the political wind wrote "30" for others, and for a variety of reasons, many papers found it impossible to live on dreams of future greatness. But in the communities where the economy prospered and the population grew, newspapers survived changes in management and name and lived on. Today there are 15 dailies and 57 weekly papers devoted to printing general news in the state of Arizona. Although this list is small compared to the number of papers in midwestern and eastern states, it is proportionately high, for Arizona today has only 60 incorporated towns. The 72 newspapers with their modern shops and services cover the field well.

As a matter of fact they were covering it well in Territorial days, but those early papers must be read with understanding of the conditions under which they were published. To begin with, they were extremely parochial. There was little interest in day-to-day news from other communities, unless it was news of disaster or an outburst of crime. Phoenix published relatively little about Tucson, and Tucson exhibited only a minor interest in Phoenix, an expression of parochialism that does not sound too unfamiliar even today. Neither Tucson nor Phoenix paid much attention to Nogales,

Flagstaff, Prescott or to other Arizona towns. Perhaps this localism reflected in part, the poorer communications of the age.

After all, the newspaper of Territorial days had a purpose. It should be remembered that every paper was the voice of its business district and of the local Chamber of Commerce. The result was steady publication of extravagant claims of growth and prosperity. Prospects for finding oil were heavily advertised. Every prospector who came in from the hills was said to have a bonanza which would make him and the town rich. Scores of tall tales told of new hotels, business blocks, national fraternal hospitals, appeared in print, but were never to be heard of again.

So flagrant and enterprising was promotion that Tucson had no sewers when *The Star* wrote a two-column story and ran it for months without changing a line, depicting the town as a health resort of world-wide fame. In like manner, Phoenix papers boasted daily of the Salt River Valley. In both towns the papers campaigned steadily for settlers. The drive for population was always of primary concern to Americans everywhere — to the land speculator, the promoter, the visionary and the hard-headed. At one time, for example, Arizonans considered trying to make a deal with California for caravans of families interested in homesteading. As for other uniform or consistent policies, almost the only ones pursued by the newspapers were control or extinction of the Indians and the necessity for more and bigger government appropriations.

Crime at home and throughout the Territory was a subject of continuing comment. Although a conscientious effort has been made in this book to avoid over-emphasis on this phase of Arizona life, crime was so widely reported in the early newspapers that it cannot be ignored. But it can and should be seen in perspective, which is the reflective quality that is perhaps most of all and most naturally lacking from the early record.

For example, by modern standards the early press was strangely remiss in failing to develop what is known as the "local tie-in." This is accomplished by first realizing that a world or national news story may and probably does have local consequences, and then writing or assigning an article on what the effect is likely to be in the local area. Early editors got around to the effects eventually, but only when they occurred or were about to occur. In extenuation it may be said that this is a weakness still discoverable in some modern newspapers.

Pioneer editors and reporters were at their best in handling straight news and personals, and it is this which makes their papers so valuable and so fascinating today. One finds an unlimited collection of newshards. Painstakingly fitted together, these fragments give an intimate and rare picture. Perspective is thus seen as the blessing of time and distance. We begin to find a cause and effect, hopes which failed or were forgotten, and small successes which, joined with others equally small, eventually brought about epochal advances. And the pioneer newsmen were especially strong in one important aspect of news coverage which makes the formation of modern perspective possible: they followed a news story to its ending, even though this took days, weeks, or months.

Best of all for us, they answered the questions we ask flying over the desert at night, or standing high in the mountains, looking down at clusters or ordered lights which are the streets of Arizona towns, or the sweeping course of roads and highways spread across wide valleys. We wonder, "What kind of people *were* they who wrought the thousands of small miracles that make up these great miracles below."

The Territorial press of Arizona gives us history's answer.

Acknowledgement must be made of the assistance of the library staff of the Arizona Pioneers Historical Society, of the efforts of Miss Phyllis Ball, director of Special Collections at the University. Particular thanks are due Mr. Donald Powell for his help and unfailing knowledge of Arizona books.

Tucson, 1963.   Douglas D. Martin

THE TERRITORIAL
YEARS 1846–1912

1846 MAY 13. President James K. Polk declares a state of war exists between The United States and Mexico. (56)

OCT. 20. Gen. Stephen W. Kearny with 300 dragoons, known as the "Army of the West," takes the Gila trail to the Yuma Crossing and on Nov. 25 crosses the Colorado River into California. (38–56)

DEC. 17. Lt. Col. Phillip St. George Cooke's Mormon Battalion takes possession of Tucson and raises American flag without encountering Mexican garrison. (38–56)

1847 JAN. 10. After making a wagon road across Arizona, the Mormon Battalion enters California over the Yuma Crossing. (38–56)

1848 FEB. 2. Treaty of Guadalupe-Hidalgo ending war with Mexico is signed. Proclaimed effective by President Polk on July 4. (1–23–39–56)

OCT. 25. U. S. First dragoons reach Tucson enroute to California. (19)

NOV. 27. First dragoons cross Colorado at Yuma. Lieut. Cave Couts was a member of this command. (38)

1849 OCT. 2. Lieut. Cave Couts establishes Camp Calhoun on hill overlooking the Yuma Crossing to protect hundreds of immigrants heading for the goldfields of California. He writes in his diary, "The immigrants, oh, the immigrants, begging sugar, flour, molasses, pork, fresh beef, rice, and coffee." (38)

OCT. 12. Charles E. Pancoast's immigrant party completes voyage down the Gila River with a child born on riverbank by a Mrs. Howard. This is first white child of record born in Arizona. Pancoast says it was a boy. Lieutenant Couts says it was a boy. Its name was "Gila." (7–38)

1850 JAN. Dr. Able Lincoln builds the first commercial ferry on the Colorado at Yuma. Sixty thousand immigrants take the southern route through Arizona to the goldfields of California this year. (38)

APRIL 23. Yuma Indians massacre ferrymen at the Yuma Crossing, killing 15. Three of the ferrymen escape and reach coastal cities. (38–56)

JULY 11. Louis J. F. (Don Diego) Jaeger and party defy Yuma Indians and launch new ferry at the Yuma Crossing. (38–39)

SEPT. 9. Congress passes the "Omnibus Bill" making Arizona and New Mexico one territory, with the proviso, "Nothing in this act shall be construed to inhibit the United States from dividing said Territory into two or more territories." (56)

NOV. 27. Capt. S. P. Heintzelman with three companies arrives at Yuma Crossing and gives name, Camp Independence, to the fort. (39)

First U. S. Census to include New Mexico places population figure at 61,547 but does not give number living in Arizona. (56)

1851 MAR. 28. Famous Oatman pioneer family reaches the Pima villages from Tucson. A few days later, Indians slaughter the parents, capture two daughters, and leave a son for dead. Bancroft says Indians were Tonto Apaches, *San Francisco Bulletin* reported they were Mohaves; Stratton, who wrote a book on it, names both tribes. (56)

SEPT. 15. Fort Defiance is established in what is now Apache County. Abandoned April 18, 1861. (16)

NOV. 11. Jaeger's ferry at Yuma Crossing is sunk and Camp Independence is attacked by Yuma Indians. Lieut. T. J. Sweeny holds out until December and then withdraws with his half-starved garrison. (38)

Mormons establish temporary settlement in Tubac. (39)

1852 FEB. 22. Maj. S. P. Heintzelman returns to Colorado River crossing with four companies of infantry and one of dragoons. Rebuilds fort. Jaeger returns and builds new ferry. (56)

AUG. 3. Eight hundred braves from the Colorado tribes attack Fort Yuma. Maj. Heintzelman's troops decisively defeat Indians. (38)

SEPT. 3. Schooner "Capacity" reaches mouth of the Colorado River and unloads steam engine, boiler, and lumber for a river steamboat. (38)

NOV. 3. Capt. Lorenzo Sitgreaves reaches Fort Yuma after making survey of the Zuni, Little Colorado, and Rio Colorado. (38–39)

DEC. 3. "Uncle Sam," first Colorado River steamboat, reaches Yuma. (38)

1853 MAR. 3. Second session of the 32nd U. S. Congress adjourns after appropriating funds for exploration and survey of a railroad route from the Mississippi to the Pacific ocean, via Holbrook and Flagstaff. (39)

DEC. 30. Under terms of the Gadsden Purchase the United States agrees to pay Mexico ten million dollars for 45,535 acres of land below the Gila River from the Rio Grande to the Colorado. Of this land, 31,535 square miles are eventually included in the Territory of Arizona. (18–56)

1854 JAN. 18. River steamer "General Jessup" appears at Yuma Crossing. (38)

JAN. 24. Lieuts. John C. Parke and George Stoneman leave San Diego and move across Yuma Crossing to the Pima Villages on the Gila where they begin survey for railroad route to Doña Ana. Arrive at destination, via Tucson, March 13. (51)

APRIL 25. Gadsden Purchase is ratified and signed by President Franklin Pierce. Becomes effective June 30. (56)

JUNE 22. First steamship disaster on the Colorado sees the "Uncle Sam" sink opposite Pilot Knob. (1–38)

AUG. 4. Congress awards lands acquired by the Gadsden Purchase to New Mexico. (57)

Arizona Copper Co., incorporates in San Francisco and begins operating the copper mine now known as the New Cornelia in Ajo. (38)

1855 JAN. 31. Wm. H. Emory, boundary commissioner, establishes initial monument on the Rio Grande, as starting point for survey of boundaries following the Gadsden Purchase. (44)

MAY 16. Maj. Henry C. Wayne ordered to Levant to purchase camels for U. S. Army use on Arizona deserts. (1)

1856 FEB. 28. Solomon Warner reaches Tucson from Yuma at head of train of 13 mules loaded with merchandise for first Arizona general store. (39)

MAR. 10. U. S. Army quarters four companies of dragoons in Tucson. (57)

MAR. 24. Charles D. Poston organizes the Sonora Exploring and Mining Co. With Maj. S. P. Heintzelman as president, he purchases the Arivaca Ranch west of Tubac and begins operation of mines. (26)

MAY 29. Camp Moore renamed Fort Buchanan. (16)

AUG. 26. Two hundred and sixty citizens of Arizona hold convention in Tucson, petition Congress to create a Territorial government, and elect Nathan B. Cook, Territorial delegate. Congress does not concur. (19)

DEC. 4. First post office in Southern Arizona is established at Fort Buchanan. (26)

1857 MAR. 1. Henry A. Crabb, commanding a band of filibusters, enters Mexico by way of Jaeger's ferry on the Colorado with the intention of conquering Sonora; Mexican militia trap the band at Caborca and wipe it out on April 6. (24)

JUNE 22. U. S. government signs contract with James E. Birch for semimonthly mail and passenger service from San Antonio to San Diego, via Tucson. Became known as the "Jackass Mail" because passengers frequently had to ride a mule between Fort Yuma and the coast. (3)

SEPT. 4. Lieut. Edward F. Beale reaches the Colorado 125 miles above Needles after surveying wagon route along the 35th parallel from Fort Defiance. He uses camels as well as mules. (52)

SEPT. 15. Government signs Overland Mail contract with John Butterfield. (1)

DEC. 8. President James Buchanan recommends to Congress that Arizona be made a Territory. Expecting passage of a Territorial bill, Tucson sends Lieut. Sylvester Mowry to Washington as a Territorial delegate; Congress rejects Buchanan's recommendation and Mowry is not seated. (1956)

1858 JAN. 2. River Steamer "General Jessup," first to navigate the Colorado above Yuma, reaches point 20 miles above Hardyville. (55)

FEB. 14. Charles D. Poston officiates at first marriage ceremony in the Territory at Tubac. (15)

JULY 5. New wagon road which by-passes Gila Desert is completed between Fort Yuma and El Paso. Typescript from *Steamer Bulletin*. (C)

SEPT. Jacob Snively, a Texan, finds gold along the Gila River above Yuma. Gila City is born, but vanishes in 1862. (38–56)

SEPT. 3. Arizona citizens meet again in convention at Tucson and petition Congress for Territorial status. Sylvester Mowry again chosen as Congressional delegate. Congress again refuses to act. (B)

OCT. 1. First Butterfield Overland Mail coach enters Arizona through Stein's Pass; reaches Tucson, Oct. 2, 6:15 p.m. and crosses into California on Jaeger's ferry, Oct. 5, 6:15 a.m.

William S. Oury introduces first herd of fine cattle to Arizona, pasturing 100 heifers and four bulls in the Santa Cruz Valley near Tucson. (44)

1859 FEB. 25. Fifty-eight residents of Territory meet at Tubac and petition Congress to establish and pay troop of Arizona Rangers. (15)

FEB. 28. Gila River Reservation is established for Pima and Maricopa Indians by Congressional Act (11 Stat. 401. c. 66 sec. 3-5). (32)

MAR. 3. *Weekly Arizonian,* first Arizona newspaper printed in Tubac. Vol. I, No. One, reports 19 acts of murder and robbery by Indians between Jan. 1 and Feb. 21. (59)

APRIL 1. Reverend Tuthill, Methodist missionary, arrives in Tubac, April 7. Holds first Protestant service in Arizona. Later he became a circuit rider, preaching in Calabasas, Fort Buchanan, Tucson, and on various Sonoita ranches. (C)

APRIL 15. Camp Colorado is established on the Colorado River as base for California-bound immigrants. One week later name is changed to Fort Mohave. Abandoned in 1861. Regarrisoned by troops from California Column, May 19, 1863. (16)

MAY 1. Father Joseph P. Machebeuf is named first American Catholic priest for Arizona and leaves Mesilla for Tucson where he converts two-room house into first American Catholic Church in June. He repairs San Xavier, making it suitable for Mass. (20)

JUNE 24. Tucson celebrates St. John's Day with cockfights, horse races, liquor and fist fights. (59)

JULY 3. Citizens of Tucson and Mesilla hold conventions naming Lieut. Sylvester Mowry delegate to Congress. No action by Congress. (59: Aug. 4)

JULY 8. Sylvester Mowry engages Edward E. Cross, editor of the *Arizonian,* in duel at Tubac. Cross had said Mowry's claims of Arizona population were false. Burnside rifles at 40 paces. No blood flows. (59)

JULY 16. Apaches raid the Sonora Exploring and Mining Co., and drive off stock valued at $7,000. (59)

AUG. 4. Lieut. Sylvester Mowry buys *Weekly Arizonian* and publishes it in Tucson. (59)

NOV. 12. Forty-six thousand sheep pass through Tucson en route to California. (59)

1860 JAN. 31. New Mexico Legislature establishes Arizona County, giving it most of the western portion of Gadsden Purchase lands. Twitchell, Ralph C. (B)

APRIL 2–5. Thirty-one citizens, meeting in Tucson, draw up a Territorial constitution which is supposed to be effective until Congress establishes a legal government. The provisions are never enforced. (59)

APRIL 5. In effort to provide basis for some kind of law provisional government sets up a supreme court in Tucson. (9)

AUG. 26. Mark A. Aldrich, Tucson business man is made alcalde [judge] of Tucson but resigns in disgust Nov. 1, because citizens refuse to make complaints about crime. (9)

The first book printed in Arizona is a 24-page pamphlet on the proceedings of the Constitutional Convention which met April 2, in Tucson. The printer is J. Howard Wells. Photostatic copy. (C)

Lieut. Sylvester Mowry buys the Patagonia Mine east of the Santa Cruz Valley·and renames it the Mowry Mine. (26)

U. S. decennial census of Arizona population given as approximately 6,482. (49)

1861 FEB. 1. Texas secedes from the Union; Congress halts Butterfield Mail, isolating Arizona. (56)

FEB. 4. Cochise, at peace with Americans, pays ceremonial visit under white flag to Second Lieut. George H. Bascom and force encamped at Apache Pass. Bascom attempts to capture Cochise who slits tent and escapes. In wild rage Cochise opens bloody Apache war which lasts twelve years with fearful toll of lives and property in Southern Arizona. (3)

MAR. 2. Congress annuls contract with Butterfield Stage and company begins destroying stations along the southern route. (46)

JULY 10. Federal troops destroy and abandon Fort Breckenridge. Re-established by troops from the California Column in 1862. Becomes Fort Grant, 1865. (16)

JULY 21. Seven men guarding a mail coach en route to Tucson and the coast are trapped in Cook's Canyon by 300 Apaches under Cochise and Mangas Coloradas. Battle lasts three days. Cochise later said he lost 125 braves before guards were wiped out. (60)

JULY 23. Fort Buchanan with military stores abandoned and burned, as U. S. troops are called east for Civil War duties. (16)

AUG. 1. Lt. Col. John R. Baylor, CSA, declares Arizona to be a Confederate Territory; all New Mexico lying south of the 34th parallel included. (56)

AUG. 3. Abandoned as Union troops move east, the residents of Tubac hold out against Indians and Mexican freebooters for three days. Escape after nightfall. (38)

AUG. 10. Declaring Arizona has been deserted by the federal government and left to the Apaches, 68 citizens hold a mass meeting in Tucson, vote to join the Confederacy and send Granville Oury to the Confederate Congress as a delegate. Oury is not seated. (Oury file: B.)

SEPT. 27. Mining village of Piños Altos attacked by war party of Indians. Arizona guards drive off marauders. (23)

1862 JAN. Pauline Weaver, the mountain man, and party find gold 10 miles above Ehrenberg on the Colorado. Town of La Paz has 5,000 inhabitants in four years and just misses being made capital of the Territory. River changes its course and La Paz vanishes after its sands give up $8 million in gold dust. (70)

JAN. 2. Floods on the Colorado and Gila wash away Colorado City and submerge entire valley between Fort Yuma and Pilot Knob. (58)

JAN. 18. Confederate Congress passes enabling act, making Arizona and New Mexico Confederate Territories; Jefferson Davis signs, Feb. 14. (56)

FEB. 28. Capt. Sherod Hunter of the Confederate army enters Tucson with 200 mounted Texans and is greeted with a celebration. (39)

MAR. 11. Marcus H. McWillie seated by Confederate Congress as delegate from Arizona. (56)

APRIL 15. Detachment of Hunter's Texans from Tucson are overtaken by scouting party of U. S. Cavalry from Yuma. Minor engagement known as "farthest West battle" of the Civil War is fought at Picacho Pass. Alerted by news that California Column is advancing, Confederate troops retreat from Tucson.

MAY 20. Advance Guard of California Column enters Tucson under Col. Joseph R. West. (56)

MAY 20. Congress passes the Homestead Act, giving free land to citizens who qualify for ownership by living on the land. (56)

JUNE 6. Military court convened by Gen. James H. Carleton at Tucson finds Lieut. Sylvester Mowry guilty of treason and imprisons him in Fort Yuma. (23)

JUNE 8. Gen. James H. Carleton, commanding the California Column, declares Arizona under martial law, and proclaims it a Territory of the government of the United States "until such time as the President of the United States shall otherwise direct." (56)

JULY 14. Advance guards of California Column's wagon train attacked by Indians under Mangas Coloradas and Cochise. Apaches driven off with loss of 60 braves. (56)

JULY 15. Apaches launch a second attack when Carleton's wagon train reaches Apache Pass and are again defeated. Carleton leaves one company of California Column at Apache Pass to protect a spring. This becomes Camp Bowie, July 26. (56)

JULY 20. Two troops from First and Second U. S. Cavalry establish a temporary post at Tubac. (3)

1863 FEB. 20. Congress passes Arizona Territorial Bill which becomes law Feb. 24. (56)

MAR. 4. President Abraham Lincoln appoints Arizona Territorial officials. John A. Gurley is named governor, dies Aug. 18. John N. Goodwin replaces him. (56)

SEPT. 13. Gen. James H. Carleton asks War Department to send him a regiment of cavalry to protect the gold fields and Camp Pomeroy, later Fort Whipple. Request denied. (23)

DEC. 29. Gov. John N. Goodwin and his official party of territorial appointees take the oath of office at Navajo Springs, and Arizona has a government. (26)

First permanent white settlement established in Maricopa County at Wickenburg. (57)

1864 JAN. 6. Col. Kit Carson with 300 men leaves Fort Canby for winter attack on stronghold of the Navajos in Canyon de Chelly. As result of Carson victory, 12,000 Navajos surrender in following months. (23)

JAN. 24. Territorial officials reach Fort Whipple and set up government. (56)

FEB. 23. King S. Woolsey, prominent pioneer, lures Tonto Apaches into peace parley at Bloody Tanks, pretending to represent President Lincoln. Feeds warriors pinole laced with strychnine and gives signal to his party to open fire on chiefs. Woolsey himself kills chief sitting at his side. Estimate of Apache dead runs from 22 to 200. (Pinole Treaty file. C.)

MAR. 9. Robert C. McCormick, Territorial Secretary of State publishes first issue of *Arizona Miner* at Fort Whipple. (56)

MAR. 11. Tonto Apaches kill three miners in the Hassayampa Canyon and continuing towards Weaver, kill five Mexicans and attack a wagon train, fatally wounding two more men. (23)

APRIL 9. Gov. John N. Goodwin issues a proclamation dividing the Territory into three judicial districts. (56)

MAY 4. The name Phoenix is made official by Yavapai supervisors establishing boundaries of precincts and naming one of them "Phoenix Precinct." (57)

MAY 8. Governor Goodwin proclaims Tucson an incorporated city and appoints officials. (19)

MAY 24. U. S. Marshal Milton B. Duffield completes the first census of Arizona and reports to Governor Goodwin that the population totals 4,573, including U. S. soldiers. Arizona had sworn to Congress that the population was 6,500. (36)

MAY 26. First Territorial proclamation is issued by Gov. John N. Goodwin. (1)

MAY 30. Territorial government moves capital from Fort Whipple to Granite Creek; citizens rename spot Prescott and 232 lots are sold by July 4. (23)

MAY 31. First district court of the First Judicial District of Arizona, called in Tucson and holds first trials under American jurisprudence. (9)

JULY 18. Territorial election of members of legislature and a delegate to Congress; Charles D. Poston. (19)

JULY 27. John B. Allen makes first application for homestead land in Arizona. (23)

SEPT. 26. First Territorial Legislature convenes in Prescott. Adopts a code of laws; creates Mohave, Yavapai, Pima, and Yuma counties; earmarks $1,500 for education from a total appropriation of $16,137; establishes a University and a Board of Regents. (31)

DEC. 2. Mormons establish Beaver Dams, first agricultural settlement in northern Arizona. Now known as Littlefield. (40)

DEC. 7. Under the act to raise money for public schools, Legislature appropriates $250 for first public school then being conducted at San Xavier by Fr. Carlos E. Messea. (31)

DEC. 17. Callville located on Colorado River by the Mormons as site of landing and warehouse. (23)

DEC. 26. Supreme Court of the Territory of Arizona holds its first session in Prescott. (9)

1865 JAN. 1. Charles Trumbull Hayden is appointed first probate judge of Pima County by Governor Goodwin. (57)

FEB. 4. Arizona transferred from U. S. Army Department of New Mexico to the Department of California. (23)

JULY 25. First Masonic Lodge (Aztlan Lodge No. One, F. & A. M.) meets in Governor's mansion. (26)

SEPT. 7. Camp Verde located on the Rio Verde River above junction with Salt River. Soon renamed Camp Lincoln. (16)

OCT. 31. Gen. John S. Mason, commanding Department of Colorado, issues order at Prescott; "All Apache Indians in this Territory are hostile and all men old enough to bear arms who are encountered will be slain wherever met unless they give themselves up as prisoners. No women and children will be harmed." (23)

DEC. 6. Second Territorial Legislature convenes in Prescott under Acting Gov. R. C. McCormick. Passes no appropriation bill, expenses being limited to support from Congress; total taxes collected are $1,155. Pima County with largest population pays $274. Yuma pays nothing. Creates Pah-Ute County from section of northern Mohave County. (31)

MAR. 1. Gilbert W. Hopkins, of first Board of Regents, and William Wrightson, first publisher of the *Arizonian* at Tubac are murdered near Fort Buchanan by Indians. (23)

MAR. 3. Congressional Act establishes the Colorado River Reservation for the Indians of the Colorado River and its tributaries. (13 Stat., 559, c. 127). (32)

Arizona is combined with Nevada, Utah and New Mexico in Episcopal Church Missionary Jurisdiction of Nevada. Bishop Whitaker visits it once. (52)

1866 MAR. 14. *Prescott Miner* reports that Arizona has never received the customary Congressional appropriation of $2,500 for foundation of a Territorial library. (70)

OCT. 3. Third Territorial Legislature convenes in Prescott under Governor McCormick. Territorial census shows population is 5,526. Governor makes gloomy report; Territory is deep in debt; there are no stagecoach lines; roads are extremely poor; Apaches are very active; total amount of taxes collected, $355. (31)

NOV. 6. Territorial Legislature asks Congress to donate 320 acres of land for Prescott townsite. (39)

DEC. 28. Rev. Charles M. Blake holds first Presbyterian Church service in Arizona in a log cabin at Prescott. (73)

Total number of cattle in Arizona, 200,000; value, $3 million. (50)

1867 JAN. 2. Fourteen Arizona Rangers under Tom Hodges attack war party of Apaches near Rock Springs and kill 21 braves. (58)

MAR. 18. Military headquarters in the Territory are moved from Prescott to Tucson. (23)

APRIL 10. Richard C. McCormick appointed governor. (56)

MAY 5. Congress gives western section of Pah-Ute County to Nevada, remaining portion is returned to Mohave County. (56)

JAN. 26. Aztlan Lodge No. I, F.&A.M. is constituted at Prescott. (52)

MAR. 3. Congress transfers Arizona from Surveying District of New Mexico to that of California. Surveying party makes headquarters at Maricopa Wells. (23)

AUG. 10. U. S. Army establishes Fort Crittenden between the settlements of Sonoita and Patagonia to protect settlers from Indians. Fort officially abandoned June 1, 1873. (16)

AUG. 29. Tucson post garrison which is stationed on Military Plaza is named Camp Lowell. (16)

SEPT. 4. Fourth Territorial Legislature convenes in Prescott; passes act making it unlawful to use weapons other than in self-defense; authorizes creation of school districts by boards of supervisors; moves the Capital from Prescott to Tucson; defeats resolution to substitute LaPaz for Tucson by vote of 9 to 7; petitions Congress to permit governor to raise regiment of cavalry. (31)

SEPT. 8. First tri-weekly mail from the East reaches Tucson, courtesy the U. S. Army. (70)

OCT. 1. Pima County members of the legislature resign during the session, leaving that body without a quorum. Action is taken as protest against a bill which would have left location of the capital to a vote of the people. (70)

NOV. 1. Tucson becomes the Capital of the Territory. (31)

Total number of all cattle in Arizona, 220,000, value, $3,520,000. (50)

1868 JAN. 1. First herd of cattle in the Salt River Valley turned out to graze near Tempe by Thomas T. Hunter. (44)

MAY 4. Supervisors of Yavapai County establish a new election precinct and name it Phoenix. (23–56)

JUNE 1. Treaty between the Navajo Indians and the United States Government sets aside lands for the Navajo Indian Reservation; establishes compulsory education for children between the ages of six and sixteen; guarantees school facilities for Navajos; causes Navajos to relinquish claims to land outside the reservation; promises clothing and certain annuities for Navajos for ten years; etc. (15 Stat., 667-672). (32)

(There have been more than 35 Executive Orders and Congressional Acts dealing with the Navajo Reservation lands since this date.)

JUNE 7. Substantial building, later to become St. Joseph's Academy for Tucson girls, is roofed with lumber cut in the Huachuca Mountains. (59)

AUG. 18. Mrs. Mary A. Gray, believed to be the first white woman in the valley north of the Salt River, arrives this date. (23)

SEPT. 25. Arizona Territory becomes a separate Roman Catholic Diocese under Bishop J. B. Salpointe. (39)

NOV. 3. First U. S. land office opens in Phoenix. (56)

Presbyterian Board of Foreign and Domestic Missions in New York reports that there is no Protestant mission or missionary in Arizona. It sends two boxes of Bibles to army wives at Fort McDowell who have started a Sunday school. Two New York churches underwrite salary of the Rev. James A. Skinner of Stockton, Calif., who leaves for Prescott in January of 1869. (70)

NOV. 10. Fifth Territorial Legislature meets under Governor McCormick who is about to become delegate to Congress. He delivers a long farewell address. Legislature concerns itself principally with memorials, Congressional help in getting a railroad and arms and ammunition for citizens, but does also pass a general school law. (31)

Total value of major metals production in Arizona $600,000. (22)

Total number of all cattle in Arizona, 235,000; value, $3,760,000. (50)

1869 FEB. 5. Apaches attack Pete Kitchen's Potrero ranch and drive off his sheep. Kitchen pursues them. (58)

MAR. 6. Twenty soldiers from Camp Lowell, drunk and armed, storm Tucson, shooting up the town and wounding one citizen. (59)

APRIL 7. Anson P. K. Safford appointed governor. (56)

APRIL 26. Express rider from the east attacked by Indians at Apache Pass. Mail captured for the third time in three months. (59)

APRIL 20. Command of 100 men from Camp Grant traps large party of Apaches. Twenty-seven braves die. (59)

MAY 24. John Wesley Powell and party begin historic exploration in boats of the Colorado River starting at headwaters of the Green River and traveling 1,555 miles to the head of the Gulf of California. (56)

SEPT. 21. Maj. Gen. George H. Thomas refuses Gov. A. P. K. Safford's offer of volunteer troops for service against the Indians. (59)

OCT. 23. Contract mail route goes into operation between Tucson, Fort Grant, Florence, Phoenix, and Camp McDowell. (59)

OCT. 9. Apaches attack army detachment guarding mails from east, 25 miles from Apache Pass. Six whites killed. (59)

DEC. 18. Mail rider dies between Florence and Camp McDowell at the hands of Indians. (59)

Total value of major metals production in Arizona, $800,000. (22)

Total number of cattle in Arizona, 250,000; value $4,006,500. (50)

1870 APRIL 4. War Department decides to arm Arizona militia and furnish rations for men on military duty. Gov. A. P. K. Safford issues a call for volunteers. (59)

MAY 26. Seven Sisters of St. Joseph finish their historical journey from San Diego to Tucson. (A)

AUG. 7. Indian depredations increase. Ten settlers are killed in eleven days. (59)

AUG. 10. Phoenix Ditch Co., makes claim to 5,000 acre inches of water from the Salt River. One day later claims additional 5,000 acre inches. (23)

SEPT. 21. Gov. A. P. K. Safford comes out of the mountains Sept. 21, at the head of the state militia after a 26-day campaign between the Santa Cruz and San Pedro rivers without having seen an Apache. (59)

SEPT. 26. Prescott Ditch Co., locates a ditch and claims 4,000 acre inches of Salt River water for irrigation.

OCT. 15. Richard C. McCormick, Congressional delegate, launches first issue of the *Arizona Citizen* in Tucson as a vehicle for personal political ideas. (59)

OCT. 20. Citizens mark out a townsite, the location of the present Phoenix. (23–56)

NOV. 17. Charles T. Hayden organizes Hayden Milling and Farming Ditch Co., and prepares to establish ferry and mill on the south side of the Salt River. This spot became Tempe. (56)

DEC. 23. Rev. Charles H. Cook, pioneer Presbyterian missionary reaches the Pima Villages and is engaged to preach and open a school. Feb. 15 he begins teaching at a salary of $1,000 a year. Hamilton, John M., Master's Thesis, 1948. University of Arizona. (A)

U. S. Census reports Arizona population as 9,658. (49)

Total value of major metals production in Arizona, $800,000. (22)

Total number of all cattle in Arizona, 250,000; value, $4,255,000.

1871 JAN. 1. Salt River Farming Ditch company claims 15,000 acre inches of Salt River water. (23)

JAN. 7. Monterey Ditch Co., claims 10,000 acre inches of Salt River water. (23)

JAN. 11. Sixth Territorial Legislature convenes in Tucson. Creates Maricopa and repeals act which created Pah-Ute County; informed by Gov. A. P. K. Safford that mining is booming but that there is not a public school in the Territory. General school act providing for support of schools is passed. Territory is reported out of debt. (31)

FEB. 15. First Indian school established at Sacaton by Rev. Charles H. Cook, a missionary teacher. (26)

FEB. 28. Phoenix is made county seat of new Maricopa County by voters. (57)

MAR. 3. The *Arizona Miner* appeals to the American people for protection from Apaches and prints three columns of names of pioneers known to have been slaughtered in seven years. (42)

APRIL 10. Under the leadership of Wm. S. Oury and three other prominent citizens of Tucson, a band of 140 Americans, Mexicans and Papagos attack a sleeping camp of Apache prisoners at Camp Grant. They shoot and club to death 83 women and children and carry 30 children off to be sold into Mexican slavery. This is the Camp Grant Massacre, the news of which shocked the nation. President Grant called it "pure slaughter" but a jury acquitted everyone concerned. (39)

MAY 17. Village of Tucson buys two sections of land from federal government and begins to sell lots and issue deeds. (7)

NOV. 5. Wickenburg stage held up and six passengers killed. Charge made that highwaymen were Mexicans disguised as Indians. (23)

NOV. 9. An executive order establishes the White Mountain Reservation, formerly set aside by the War Department as an Indian reservation for Apaches. (32)

NOV. 10. First homestead entry in Arizona filed at Prescott by Nathan Bowers. (26)

DEC. 6. Military telegraph line reaches Tucson. Town celebrates with grand ball. (26–74)

DEC. 10. First sale of lots in Phoenix authorized. (56)

DEC. 16. *Prescott Miner* reports first important flour mill (the Helling Mill) in operation in Phoenix. Mill supplies Army posts north of the Gila and has agencies in Prescott, Wickenburg, Maricopa Wells, Florence, and Tucson. (23)

Presbyterian Church establishes mission for the Pimas near Tucson. (57)

Major metals production in Arizona $800,000. (22)

Total number of cattle in Arizona 265,000; value, $4,246,000. (50)

1872 FEB. 13. First American couple married in Phoenix; principals, George Buck and Miss Matilda Murray. (23)

FEB. 19. Farmers take out North Extension Ditch of the Swilling Canal. (23)

MAR. 4. First public school opens in Tucson. (19)

MAR. 10. First edition of *Arizona Sentinel* appears at Yuma. (35)

MAR. 24. Tucson citizens lynch four outlaws in front of the jail house. (42)

MAY 7. First lawyers are admitted to practice law in Maricopa County. (23)

JUNE 24. Having built bridge across Little Colorado River, settlers name townsite St. Johns. (26)

JULY 30. Corporation is formed in San Francisco to develop diamond fields in Northern Arizona. Swindle becomes known as the *Great Diamond Hoax*. Harpending, Asbury. (C)

SEPT. 5. First public school in Phoenix opens in building known as the courthouse. (56)

SEPT. 22. Lieut. Col. George Crook files report to Military Headquarters of the Pacific detailing 154 cases of Indian depredations in Arizona between Sept. 1, 1871 and Sept. 4, 1872. Record shows three army men and 41 citizens killed, 16 citizens wounded, 554 cattle stolen. (52)

OCT. 12. In negotiations lasting from Oct. 1 to Oct. 12, Gen. O. O. Howard and Cochise, famed chief of the Chiricahua Apaches, draft and sign a peace treaty in camp near Dragoon Springs. (A)

DEC. 14. An executive order adds the San Carlos Division to the White Mountain Reservation which had previously been established. (32)

DEC. 16. Florence opens the first good school building in Arizona. (74)

Safford settled by Americans from Gila Bend and named for third Territorial Governor. (26)

Total value of major metals production in Arizona, $625,000. (22)

Total number of cattle in Arizona, 290,000; value, $4,646,000. (50)

1873 JAN. 6. Seventh Territorial Legislature convenes in Tucson. First act passed gives Gov. A. P. K. Safford a divorce; changes name of Arizona City to Yuma and provides for incorporation; asks Congress to promote sinking of artesian wells; learns from Governor average daily attendance in public schools is 400. (31)

MAR. 19. Tucson garrison is moved to site on Rillito Creek, and important permanent post is built and named Fort Lowell. Abandoned April 10, 1891. (16)

MAY 2. Yuma holds its first legal hanging across the road from the schoolhouse. (26)

MAY 29. Troop from Fifth Cavalry establishes camp on San Carlos River near the Gila. It becomes headquarters for military government of San Carlos Indian Agency. Closed by the Army in July, 1900. (16)

JULY 3. Phoenix Vigilantes hang thief for theft of widow's cow. (39)

AUG. 6. Law and Order Society of Tucson lynches four murderers from gallows in Court Plaza on Pennington Street. (19)

OCT. 15. John L. Blythe builds and launches first large ferry at Lee's Crossing. (40)

NOV. 11. Telegraph line is completed between Yuma and Prescott. (56)

NOV. 22. An executive order enlarges the boundaries of the Colorado River Indian Reservation. (32)

DEC. 1. Wild fight develops in Third District Court room in Prescott over water rights litigation. Attorney General and District attorney engage in fist fight. P. McAteer, defendant, draws knife, stabs two litigants and is finally fatally wounded.

Congress votes $50,000 for building a military telegraph line from San Diego, via Yuma and Maricopa Wells to Prescott and Tucson. (74)

Total value of major metals production in Arizona, $500,000. (22)

Total number of all cattle in Arizona, 300,000; value, $4,505,000. (50)

1874 JAN 4. Seven Indian bands under Apache chief Eskiminzin break out of San Carlos Agency, attack a wagon train and kill two drovers. (74)

FEB. 3. Apaches escape from San Carlos Agency and attack residents of old Camp Grant agency, killing five. (74)

APRIL 4. Rev. G. A. Reader, Methodist missionary, organized a Bible class of three in Phoenix. It was the cornerstone of the first Methodist church in the city. (64)

JUNE 8. Cochise, famous chief of the Chiricahua Apaches, dies in his tribe's stronghold in the Dragoon Mountains. (18)

JUNE 24. First postmistress appointed in Arizona is Miss Jane Oswald. Office at Walnut Grove, Yavapai County. (26)

JULY 1. Executive order sets aside the San Xavier Indian reservation for use of the Papago tribe. (16)

AUG. 8. Jackson McCracken makes rich silver strike in Mohave County. The McCracken mine yields $800,000 between 1875 and 1906. (21)

SEPT. 28. *Tucson Citizen* announces first cotton grown near Tucson by Steven Ochoa. (74)

NOV. 14. Rooms are cleaned and cleared in former U. S. commissary department at Tucson for session of the Territorial Legislature. (74)

NOV. 16. An executive order enlarges the boundaries of the Colorado River Indian Reservation. (32)

NOV. 17–18. Yuma reports earthquake shocks. (74)

DEC. 19. After two trials, J. T. Holmes is convicted of killing M. B. Duffield, former U. S. Marshal, and sentenced to three years imprisonment. (74)

DEC. 26. Citizens of Arizona, California, and New Mexico petition Postmaster General for daily mail service from San Diego to Mesilla. (74)

Total value of major metals production in Arizona $590,000. (22)

Total number of cattle in Arizona, 320,000; value, $4,484,000. (50)

1875 JAN. 6. Eighth Legislature convenes in Tucson under Governor Safford. Reward of $3,000 offered for discovery of first artesian water; net profits of mines taxed; Pinal County created. County assessors' reports place population at 11,480. (31)

JAN. 9. Maricopa reports that Indians are making a practice of stealing stock from freighters and returning it for $2 to $8 a head. (74)

MAR. 22. Silver King mine discovered in Pinal Mountains. First ore assayed at $4,300 a ton. (21)

APRIL 17–27. First camp meeting held near Prescott by Methodist church. First authorized Protestant church in state is built. (23–26)

OCT. 2. Bandits hold up stage between Phoenix and Florence and take $1400. (74)

NOV. 27. Citizens of Tucson give dancing party and raise $1675 for support of public school. (74)

DEC. 7. John Clark brings first flock of sheep into Arizona via Hardy's ferry. (39)

DEC. 8. Indians stampede herd of 5,000 sheep at Maricopa, kill 20, and collect five more from drover for rounding up the flock. (74)

Annual report on public instruction shows 2,953 children of school age in the territory, half of whom cannot read or write and only 1,213 attending the short school terms. (13)

Major metals production in Arizona $954,300. (22)

Total number of all cattle in Arizona, 340,000; value, $4,425,000. (50)

1876 JAN. 30. Colorado River steamers cease landing at La Paz, which is in grip of violent smallpox epidemic. (74)

FEB. 17. United Verde Mine is located. United Verde Company incorporation takes place in 1882. (21)

MARCH 20. Proposal to disincorporate Village of Tucson is defeated at the polls. (74)

MAR. 23. Under orders to establish a mission in Northern Arizona, Mormons arrive at Sunset Crossing on Little Colorado. Create Little Colorado Mission, southeast of the crossing. (Mission records, Special Collections). (A)

APRIL 9. Dr. Sheldon Jackson establishes Presbyterian Church in Tucson. It is the first Protestant church in Southern Arizona. (Judie Moses unpublished document.) (C)

APRIL 10. Chiricahua Apaches jump reservation, kill two station keepers at Sulphur Springs, murder one San Pedro rancher and wound another. (74)

APRIL 28. Cornerstone of Territorial prison is laid at Yuma. First prisoners received in June. Institution becomes infamous as "The Hell Hole of Arizona." (23–26)

MAY 15. An executive order enlarges the boundaries of the Colorado River Reservation. (31)

JUNE 11. Chiracahua Apaches are moved from their reservation to San Carlos. (74)

JULY 1. Territorial prison completed at Yuma. (6)

JULY 4. Immigrants from Boston celebrate holiday among the pines near San Francisco Mountains and name the site Flagstaff. (26)

JULY 14. Renegade Chiracahuas kill two prospectors in Pinery Canyon south of Fort Bowie. (74)

JULY 22. Cost of feeding prisoners at penitentiary in Yuma reported to be 39 cents a day each. (74)

AUG. 12. Camp Thomas activated. Renamed Fort Thomas Feb. 11, 1882. Command withdrawn Dec. 3, 1892. Land reverts to Department of the Interior. (16)

AUG. 31. Lands are added to Gila River Reservation by an executive order. (32)

OCT. 2. Two-week Protestant camp meeting held in Phoenix by a Rev. Hedgepath. (74)

Richard J. Hinton, author of *Handbook to Arizona* claims there were 13,000 mining claims in Arizona this year.

Major metals production in Arizona $1,010,000. (22)

Total number of cattle in Arizona, 350,000; value $4,208,000 (50)

1877 JAN. 11. Ninth Territorial Legislature convenes under Governor Safford. Returns state capital to Prescott, authorizes governor to enlist a company of volunteers to hunt marauding Indians and provides for building roads from Phoenix to Globe, Prescott, Wickenburg, Agua Caliente, and Yuma. Passes net proceeds law on profits of mines. (31–57)

FEB. 5. Renegade Chiracahua Apaches murder four settlers near Sopori. (74)

FEB. 7. City of Tucson incorporated by legislative enactment. (39)

FEB. 12. Secretary of War orders 500 surplus muskets, bayonets, belts, and 25,000 ball cartridges placed at disposal of Governor Safford. (74)

FEB. 19. Gen. A. V. Kautz ignores order to equip Arizona volunteers. Pressed by Governor Safford, he reports only 90 muskets are available. (74)

MAR. 1. *Arizona Star* begins publication in Tucson as *The Bulletin*. (35)

MAR. 3. Camp Huachuca established. One of a system of posts protecting the border. Made permanent camp in 1881 and re-named Fort Huachuca. (16)

MAR. 9. Congress passes Desert Land Act which permits settler to get title to 640 acres of desert land, provided that he irrigates it within three years and pays small sum per acre. (56)

MAR. 24. Governor Safford lashes Gen. A. V. Kautz in six-column letter to *Tucson Citizen* for failing to move effectively against renegade Apaches who are terrorizing southern Arizona. (74)

APRIL 5. John P. Hoyt appointed fourth Territorial Governor. (31)

APRIL 15. Capt. William A. Hancock files first claim to desert land in Arizona. (56)

APRIL 21. Forty of John P. Clum's Apache scouts from San Carlos and a detachment of U. S. troops cross New Mexico border and raid Chiricahua hideout in Hot Springs reservation. Four hundred and twenty-seven renegade Indians, dismounted and disarmed, are marched to San Carlos with 17 leaders in chains. (74)

MAY. Teachers meet in Prescott and organize Territorial Teachers' Institute. (74)

JULY 1. John P. Clum, Indian agent at San Carlos resigns his post after long and stormy battle with the military. (74)

AUG. 2. John Dunn, government scout, finds first ore in the Bisbee district and with Lieut. J. A. Rucker and T. D. Burns files a location notice. They hire George Warren, a dissolute prospector, to work the claim. (39)

AUG. 5. An executive order restores a portion of the White Mountain Reservation to public domain. (16)

SEPT. 3. Ed. Scheffelin records first Tombstone silver claim. (1)

Governor reports to Secretary of Interior that gold and silver mines produced $5,771,555. Total assessed valuation of all property in the Territory $5,771,555. (A)

Major metals production in Arizona $1,137,500. (22)

Total number of cattle in Arizona, 375,000; value, $4,509,000. (50)

1878 JAN. 26. First Phoenix newspaper, *Salt River Herald,* begins publication. (35)

FEB. C. T. Rogers starts ranch and builds home on 160 acres at the foot of Bill Williams mountain. It becomes the city of Williams. (57)

MAR. 15. U. S. Marshal hangs soldier convicted of murder in Prescott. (72)

JUNE 8. John C. Frémont, "The Pathfinder," is appointed governor of Arizona. (C)

JUNE 13. Cornerstone of church edifice is laid in Tucson by the Presbyterian Society. The First Presbyterian Church bought this property in 1883. (60)

JULY 27. First home laundry in the Salt River Valley established in Phoenix. (72)

OCT. 8. Southern Pacific gets charter from Territory of Arizona, and then permission to cross military reservation at Yuma. (77)

NOV. 16. First brick building in Phoenix approaches completion. (72)

DEC. 21. Tempe farmer produces 6,000 pounds of sugar plus large quantity of syrup from 10 acres of sugar cane. (72)

SEPT. 28. Erastus Snow and Wm. J. Flake found the Mormon town of Snowflake. It became the first county seat of Apache County in 1879. (40)

Arizona Silver Belt established in Globe. (35)

Major metals production in Arizona $1,865,000. (22)

Total number of all cattle in Arizona, 339,000; value, $4,692,000. (50)

1879 JAN. 6. Tenth Territorial Legislature convenes under Gov. John C. Frémont. Strip is cut from eastern boundary of Yavapai, north of the Gila, to create Apache County, gambling is legalized with a $1,200 license. Legislature provides for a $31,250 lottery but postal authorities bar it from mails. (31)

JAN. First bank opens in Southern Arizona at Tucson, under the name of "Pima County Bank." (74)

JAN. 10. Lands are added to Gila River Reservation by executive order. (32)

MAR. 22. Wagon road is completed between Maricopa and Phoenix. (72)

JUNE 7. Board of Supervisors of Maricopa County appropriate $25,000 for a courthouse. Argument over location so bitter that board lets the matter die. (72)

JUNE 14. Executive order sets aside lands for Salt River Reservation for Pima and Maricopa Indians. (32)

JUNE 18. First ice plant in Arizona goes into production in Phoenix. (72)

AUG. 16. Stages between Maricopa and Phoenix are held up with such regularity that Acting Gov. John W. Gosper offers bounty of $500 for every highwayman caught in the act. (72)

AUG. 22. Law and Order Committee takes two men convicted of murder from the jail and hangs them in the Phoenix plaza. (72)

SEPT. 16. Rev. R. A. Windes, first Baptist missionary to Arizona, arrives in Prescott. He built seven Baptist churches. (C) Baptist folder.

SEPT. 23. Public shower bathhouse opens in Tucson. (60)

OCT. 2. First issue of *The Nugget* published in Tombstone. (35)

OCT. 12. First Methodist Church organized in Tucson by Supt. George H. Adams. (60)

OCT. 10. *Star* reports Tucson streets are being graded by a chain gang. (60)

DEC. 2. *Arizona Weekly Star* describes Tombstone as a town of 1,000 to 1,500 people. (44–60)

Survey of the Territory shows public schools in operation in Yuma, Ehrenberg, Mineral Park, Cerbat, Prescott, Williamson Valley, Verde, Walnut Creek, Walnut Grove, Chino Valley, Kirkland Valley, Peeples' Valley, Wickenburg, Phoenix, Florence, Tucson, Tres Alamos and Safford. Survey also shows Catholic schools at Tucson and Yuma and Indian schools at San Carlos and Sacaton. (39)

Major metals production in Arizona $2,224,500. (22)

Total number of cattle in Arizona, 430,000; value $5,180,000. (50)

1880 MAR. 20. First train over Southern Pacific reaches Tucson and is greeted by roar of cannon and a wild celebration. (19–56)

MAY 1. John P. Clum prints the first issue of the *Tombstone Epitaph* in a tent. (78)

MAY 1. Rev. Wm. H. Hill appointed first Episcopal Missionary Bishop of Arizona. Jenkins, James R. (A)

JUNE 8. An executive order reserves lands, the Havasupai Reservation, for the "Suppai" Indians. (32)

JUNE 24. Catholics begin building largest church in Arizona at Phoenix and Bishop Salpointe promises them a permanent priest when structure is dedicated. (69)

JULY 4. George Warren bets his interest in Copper Queen Mine on race against a horse and loses. His share became worth $20,000,000. (17)

AUG. 27. *Phoenix Herald* advises its readers that "without doubt cotton can be grown in the Salt River Valley.' (69)

SEPT. 10. Executive order establishes Fort Mohave Reservation. Order revoked Nov. 23 and other lands reserved for Suppai Indians. Second executive order revoked and still other lands reserved for the Suppai. (32)

SEPT. 19. An executive order establishes the Fort Mohave Indian Reservation. (32)

SEPT. 26. First Congregational Church in Arizona Territory is established at Phoenix with 13 members. (52)

OCT. 3. President Rutherford B. Hayes on grand circle tour of the nation stops at Maricopa to confer with Indian chiefs. Gen. William T. Sherman accompanying the party hears the remark that all Arizona needs is less heat and more water. Sherman replies, "Huh! That's all Hell needs." (39)

OCT. 4. John N. Irwin named governor of Arizona. (31)

OCT. 26. *Arizona Gazette* established at Phoenix. Later renamed *Phoenix Gazette*. (52)

NOV. 5. Work of erecting a Catholic church begins in Phoenix. (68)

NOV. 21. The Rev. George K. Dunlop is consecrated Episcopal bishop for New Mexico and Arizona. He builds churches in Phoenix and Tombstone. (39)

NOV. 23. An executive order revokes the executive order of June 8, 1880, and reserves other lands in Arizona for the Suppai Indians. (32)

NOV. 27. One killed in holdup of stage on Black Canyon road in Yavapai County. (60)

DEC. 10. First railway mail service in Territory established between Tucson and Los Angeles. (72)

U. S. census reports Arizona population as 40,440, a gain of 318.7 percent in 10 years. (49)

Average daily attendance in public schools 3,854. (13)

DEC. 31. Major metals production in Arizona $4,217,000. (22)

Total number of all cattle in Arizona, 475,000; value, $5,736,000. (50)

1881 JAN. 1. Tucson, Yuma, and Tombstone connected with all points east and west by telegraph lines along route of the Southern Pacific. (60)

JAN. 3. Eleventh Territorial Legislature convenes under Governor Frémont. Repeals act providing for taxation of the net profit of mines, known as the "bullion law"; creates Cochise, Graham, and Gila Counties by carving up Pima, Maricopa, and Yavapai Counties. (31)

JAN. 19. Services held in newly finished Catholic Church in Tombstone. (20)

FEB. 18. The Forty-sixth Congress grants 46,086 acres each to the Territories of Arizona, Montana, Idaho, Wyoming and Dakota for the use of universities when the Territories become states. (5)

FEB. 25. Phoenix is incorporated. Census of 1880 gives it a population of 1,780. (56)

MAR. 6. Building of Methodist church begun in Tucson under Rev. G. H. Adams. (60)

MAR. 10. Charles H. Lord, early merchant and postmaster, organizes a telephone company in Tucson. *Arizona Star* announces it has installed a telephone. (60)

MAR. 25. Water appears in the rich silver mines of Tombstone. (80)

APRIL 7. First Baptist Church of Southern Arizona organized in Tucson. (60)

JUNE 23. Barrel of whiskey explodes in Tombstone saloon and starts fire which destroys business section. (78)

JUNE 27. Thirty thousand pounds of gun powder explode in Zeckendorf powder magazine at edge of Tucson smashing windows, dishes and damaging buildings in the town. (69)

JUNE 28. Dr. James Douglas begins development of Atlanta copper claim for Phelps Dodge Co. (21) This is combined with the Copper Queen in August, 1885, and becomes Copper Queen Consolidated Mining Co.

JULY 1. Atlantic and Pacific Railroad enters Arizona. (52)

JULY 14. Tucson has first legal hanging in Pima County. (60)

AUG. 6. Cloudburst in Hassayampa Canyon destroys 20,000 pounds of freight destined for Phoenix merchants. (68)

SEPT. 16. Citizens of Phoenix hold mass meeting in the Plaza, denounce government handling of Indian problem, and raise the cry, "Removal or death for the Apache." (69)

SEPT. 19. Mass meeting in Tucson passes resolution and memorializes Congress to remove all Apaches to Indian Territory. (69)

OCT. 26. Earps, Clantons, and McLowrys stage battle at O.K. Corral in Tombstone. Three die, two wounded, in 30 seconds. (78)

DEC. 28. Marshal Virgil Earp of Tombstone shot in the back on the street and crippled for life. (78)

Four churches hold regular services in Tucson this year. Catholics worship in St. Augustine church which was built in 1869; Baptists are building but meet in courthouse; Presbyterians use an adobe building on west side of courthouse; Episcopalians use Presbyterian church while building. (74)

Citizen carries notices of meetings of Masons, Oddfellows, and the Knights of Pythias this year. (74)

City of Tombstone, Cochise County, incorporates. (34)

DEC. 31. Major metals production in Arizona $9,260,000. (22)

Total number of cattle in Arizona, 520,000; value, $7,322,000. (50)

1882 JAN. 21. *Arizona Champion,* first published at Peach Springs is transferred to Flagstaff and becomes the *Coconino Sun.* (35)

FEB. 6. Frederick A. Tritle appointed governor. (56)

MAR. 19. Morgan Earp killed from ambush in Tombstone. (78)

MAR. 21. Wyatt Earp, Doc Holliday, and party ride out of Tombstone never to return. (78)

MAR. 31. An executive order revokes the executive order of November 23, 1880, and reserves other lands in Arizona for the "Yavapai Suppai" Indians. (32)

APRIL 27. Services of Phoenix Guards offered to Governor Tritle for campaign against the Indians. (68)

MAY 3. President Chester A. Arthur warns Arizona that he will place it under martial law unless it shows more respect for law and order. Warning is directed chiefly at Cochise County. (78)

MAY 5. Lands are added to Gila River Indian Reservation by executive order. (32)

MAY 22. Saloon fire destroys business section of Tombstone again. (78)

JUNE 3. *Tucson Citizen* announces Sheriff Paul's failure to extradite Earps and "Doc" Holliday from Colorado. (74)

JUNE 4. *Arizona Daily Star* charges papers asking the Governor of Colorado to extradite the Earps and "Doc" Holliday were deliberately drawn with legal escape clauses. (60)

JUNE 18. The Rev. Endicott Peabody holds the first service in St. Paul's Episcopal Church, Tombstone. St. Paul's was the first Episcopal Church built in the Territory and was not completed at the time of the service. (52–78)

JUNE 24. Nat Greer and a party of Texas cowboys stage a wild street battle with the Mexican population of St. Johns. Two are killed. (40)

JULY 23. Mormon settlement known as Tempe is founded after purchase of 80 acres of land for $3,000 from Charles T. Hayden, pioneer merchant, miller, and ferryman. (40)

AUG. 23. Globe citizens hang two killers from tree in village street. (39)

SEPT. 11. Bisbee miners halt work to lynch a drunken killer. (39)

OCT. 29. Tucson *Weekly Citizen* reports brick is beginning to replace adobe as building material. (74)

OCT. 23. Seven notorious criminals escape from county jail in Tucson. Jail noted for similar episodes. (74)

DEC. 12. An executive order sets aside the Gila Bend Indian Reservation for use of Papago Indians. (32)

DEC. 16. Executive order sets aside certain lands for Moqui (Hopi) Indian Reservation (32)

DEC. 31. Major metals production in Arizona $11,113,023. (22)

Total number of cattle in Arizona, 570,000; value, $10,861,000. (50)

1883 JAN. 4. Executive order establishes the Hualapai Indian Reservation. (32)

JAN. 5. Fire originating in a Prescott saloon does $90,000 damage to business section. (68)

JAN. 8. Twelfth Territorial Legislature meets with Gov. F. A. Tritle. He deplores lawlessness, especially in Cochise County. Laws are written stipulating that fines from vice and gambling will be used to support schools; amendments to the general school law pass; Maricopa County is authorized to issue bonds for a courthouse. Carrying deadly weapons in villages, towns or cities is again made illegal. (31)

MAR. 17. Maricopa and Prescott mail stage is held up near Bumble Bee station and the Wells, Fargo box taken. (68)

MAR. 27. James Addison Reavis files a claim in the office of the Surveyor General in Tucson to the "Peralta Grant" which spreads 235 miles east and west and 75 miles north and south — 12 million acres of the richest lands, towns, and mines in Arizona. (45)

MAY 5. Pima County Supervisors subsidize the Narrow Gauge Railway Co., with $200,000 bond issue for road to Globe. It proves to be a gigantic swindle. (A; Bulletin No. 5)

JUNE 27. Black Canyon stage robbed. (68)

JULY 1. Black Canyon stage robbed second time in three days. (68)

JULY 21. Two Black Canyon stage robbers caught. One turns out to be village blacksmith at Gillett. (68)

AUG. 12. Florence–Globe stage and Prescott–Ash Fork stage robbed on same night. Wells, Fargo messenger on Florence–Globe run is killed. (68)

AUG. 18. The *Arizona Silver Belt* of Miami announces that work is actually underway on a railroad tunnel which will run from the Mogollon Rim to the Tonto Basin, connecting Flagstaff and Globe. The great scheme died in 1887. (3)

OCT. 4. Two Globe–Florence stage robbers are killed in gun battle with sheriff and posse. (68)

NOV. 15. Lands of Gila River Reservation are consolidated and added to by an executive order. (32)

DEC. 1. Third District Court meeting in Prescott becomes scene of wild battle when attorney general and his assistant fight with attorney for litigants in case involving water rights. P. McAteer, the defendant, stabs two litigants and is mortally wounded. (68)

DEC. 8. Five so-called "cowboys" rob Bisbee store and shoot up the town killing four citizens. Their leader is taken from county jail at Tombstone and lynched. (39–78)

DEC. 23. Salt River rises 14 feet after prolonged rainfall. Dam and headgate of the Grand Canal torn out. (68)

W. J. Sanderson of Sulphur Springs finds artesian water and receives Territorial reward of $3,000. (31)

Felix G. Hardwick wins award of $500 offered by legislature for first bale of cotton raised in Arizona. It is grown near Tempe. (26–39)

Smallpox epidemic in the Salt River Valley so severe this year that public gatherings are banned, and sheriff is given deputies to ride the roads and turn back persons who have been exposed in their home communities. (57)

DEC. 31. Major metals production in Arizona $9,353,369. (22)

Total number of cattle in Arizona, 625,000; value, $12,588,000. (50)

1884 JAN. 13. Black Canyon stage robbed near Gillett. (68)

JAN. 20. Wickenburg stage robbed near Prescott. (68)

JAN. 31. Arizona Pioneers' Historical Society organized in Tucson on call from Charles D. Poston. (31)

FEB. 7. Citizens' committee calls on people of Salt River Valley to join association and fight claims of James Addison Reavis to 7,500 square miles of Arizona's richest lands and mines. (69)

MAR. 27. Grand Lodge of Knight of Pythias is organized in Tombstone. (78)

MAR. 28. Five Bisbee bandits are hanged simultaneously at Tombstone from one gallows. (78)

APRIL 21. Black Canyon stage held up near Soap Springs. (68)

MAY 9. Powder magazine on outskirts of Phoenix explodes. Shock shatters windows in town. (69)

MAY 14. First Arizona Industrial Exposition organized in Phoenix. (39)

JUNE 1. Black Canyon stage held up and robbed. (68)

OCT. 18. Highwaymen rob travelers on Black Canyon road and hold up stage again. (68)

DEC. 31. Major metals production in Arizona $8,268,465. (22)

Total number of cattle in Arizona, 690,000; value, $14,570,000. (50)

1885 MAR. 10. Thirteenth Territorial Legislature meets with Governor Tritle, gives Phoenix $100,000 for an asylum; Tucson $25,000 for a University if it will furnish the campus free; Tempe captures $5,000 for a teacher's college and Florence is given $12,000 for a bridge. This legislature was so noted for reckless spending that it was named the "Thieving Thirteenth." (31)

APRIL 11. Largest assemblage in the history of Florence meets and organizes to fight James Addison Reavis and his claim to "The Barony of Arizona." (45)

APRIL 24. Citizens of Holbrook lynch two killers. (39)

OCT. 18. C. Meyer Zulich is appointed governor of Arizona, and takes office Nov. 22. (C)

NOV. 15. First through passenger train leaves San Diego, over Santa Fe lines along the 35th parallel across Arizona to the Mississippi valley. (56)

Phelps-Dodge partners buy interest of the largest holders of the Copper Queen mine in August, merge it with their Atlanta mine and some contiguous claims; launch the Copper Queen Consolidated Mining Company. (17)

Report on public education shows 87 school buildings, 150 schools, and a daily attendance of 3,226. Children not attending public schools number 4,151. (13)

DEC. 31. Major metals production in Arizona $6,477,287. (22)

Total number of cattle in Arizona, 750,000; value, $15,088,000. (50)

1886 JAN. 30. *Salt River Valley News* established in Tempe. Became *Tempe News,* Sept. 1887. (35)

FEB. 4. Dennis W. Dilda is hanged for murder in Prescott after a breakfast of breaded spring chicken, cream sauce, fried oysters, lamb chops, green peas, tenderloin steak with mushrooms, English pancake with jelly, potatoes, bread, and coffee. (70)

FEB. 8. Tempe Normal School opens with 33 students. Hiram B. Farmer made first president. (28)

MAR. 29. After surrendering to General Crook, Geronimo and 20 of his best warriors escape from U. S. Troops. (69)

APRIL 12. General Nelson A. Miles arrives at Bowie Station and proceeds to Fort Bowie where he replaces General Crook and opens new campaign against the Apaches. Miles Personal Recollections. (A)

APRIL 23. Disastrous fire breaks out in Phoenix and destroys a block of business buildings. Town has no fire department and no water works. (69)

MAY 21. Tucson citizens claim 100 men, women, and children have been killed by Geronimo's Apaches and appeal to Governor Zulich to do something about the raids. (69)

MAY 12. Fire destroys Grand Central pumphouse at Tombstone and mines are flooded. Operations cease. (78)

AUG. 12. Fire destroys block of 14 business houses in Phoenix. Damage $100,000. (69)

AUG. 25. Accompanied only by two friendly Chiricahuas, Lieut. Charles B. Gatewood enters Apache camp in the Sierra Madre Mountains south of the border and persuades Chief Geronimo to surrender to Gen. Nelson A. Miles. (39)

NOV. 27. Board of Regents of the University meets and accepts gift of 40 acres of land for a campus which Regent J. S. Mansfeld has persuaded two gamblers and a saloon keeper to present.

DEC. 31. Total major minerals production in Arizona, $5,441,928. (22)

Total number of cattle in Arizona, 800,000; value, $15,239.000. (50)

1887 JAN. 1. Governor Zulich drives the golden spike and completes the tracks of the Prescott and Arizona railroad. Detachment from Fort Whipple fires 100 gun salute. (70)

JAN. 19. Flagstaff mob breaks in jail doors and kills two prisoners being held on charge of murder. (79)

JAN. 24. First donation for building of Mormon Temple at Mesa. (40)

JAN. 28. Two masked men stage first train holdup in Arizona history and are reported to have taken $20,000 from Southern Pacific passenger train 17 miles east of Tucson. (40)

MAR. 8. Sheepmen start private war against cattlemen in the Tonto Basin after 20,000 head of sheep are stampeded by cowboys. (74)

MAR. 10. Fourteenth Territorial Legislature meets with Gov. C. Meyer Zulick who announces that there are 130 school districts in Arizona and 13 new school houses were built the previous year. This legislature gave the Governor power to veto sections of the appropriation bill and provided for the printing of Territorial laws. County system of establishing cattle brands is established. (31 and U.A. Bulletin No. 20)

MAY 12. *Tombstone Epitaph* reports volcano erupts in Dragoon mountains following severe earthquake. (78)

JULY 3. First railway line to Phoenix, the Maricopa and Phoenix, begins operation. (56)

AUG. 5. Executive order restores portion of White Mountain Reservation to public domain. (32)

SEPT. 4. C. P. (Commodore Perry) Owens, sheriff of Apache County, shoots four members and kills two of the Graham crowd, participants in the bloody feud over the incursion of sheep into the area. (70)

SEPT. 8. Grahams avenge their dead by killing two members of the Tewksbury faction. (70)

SEPT. 29. Southern Pacific reaches the Colorado at Yuma. (39)

SEPT. 18. Grahams ambush Tewksbury home. Three Grahams and two Tewksburys wounded. (70)

OCT. 27. Ground is broken at Tucson for the University of Arizona. (36)

NOV. 8. Gen. Nelson A. Miles visits Tucson; receives a hero's welcome and a $1,000 ceremonial sword. (74)

NOV. 19. Boiler in Prescott sawmill explodes, killing six workmen. (70)

DEC. 31. Total major minerals production in Arizona, $6,164,424. (22)

Total number of cattle in Arizona, 875,000; value, $15,923.000. (50)

1888 JAN. 17. Speaking at the first council meeting of the year Mayor Stevens of Tucson warns members that they must be prepared to do something about watering the city streets in the summer months. (74)

JAN. 17. First Pullman train rolls into Tucson and citizens turn out to marvel at the wonder. (74)

JAN. 23. Prescott public schools find themselves without funds and are forced to close. (74)

FEB. 22. Two holdup men halt westbound passenger train at Stein's Pass and rob express car. Irritated, Southern Pacific and Wells Fargo offer rewards of $2,000. Cochise sheriff takes trail leading into Mexico and is jailed there for two weeks. (74)

MAR. 19. Three guards from Vulture mine are killed on road to Phoenix and bar of gold is stolen. (74)

JUNE 1. Pete Gabriele and Joe Phy duel to the death with six-guns over politics in Florence saloon. (69)

JUNE 24. Kingman, county seat of Mohave County, is destroyed by fire. (69)

JUNE 28. Ostrich farm opened at Phoenix by M. E. Clanton. (69)

JULY 1. Fire destroys 13 buildings in Prescott. (60)

AUG. 15. Outlaws lynch three men in Holbrook in aftermath of Pleasant Valley war. (69)

OCT. 23. Highwayman holds up Jerome stage singlehanded. Six passengers yield $30. (60)

OCT. 31. Urged by Arizona Territorial Cattle Assn., federal government declares Sonora cattle are diseased and quarantines the border. Citizens claim it is a scheme to raise price of Arizona beef. (60)

NOV. 22. Florence Stage held up. Two robbers get Wells, Fargo box and $26. (60)

NOV. 22. Sacaton Indian School at Florence is destroyed by fire. (60)

DEC. 20. Work is begun on bridge across the Colorado at Needles. (60)

DEC. 24. Hold-up industry continues. Solomon and Bowie stage is robbed of mail sacks. (60)

DEC. 31. Production of gold and silver drops slightly to $3 million, and copper rises to $5,300.000. The precious metals never again equalled copper. (21)

Governor reports valuation of taxable property has risen to $30 million. (A)

Total number of cattle in Arizona, 925,000; value, $16,237,000. (50)

1889 JAN. 7. Three Mexican sheepmen are killed in a fight with cowmen near Solomonville. (74)

JAN. 14. First Mormon academy is founded in St. Johns. (40)

JAN. 29. Fifteenth Territorial Legislature meets in Prescott and votes to move capital to Phoenix, adjourns and reconvenes in Phoenix, Feb. 7. Governor Zulick delivers his message but his term expires before session ends and Lewis Wolfley takes over. Zulick hid 11 acts in a drawer of his desk, one of which was a compulsory school law. (31)

JAN. Bishop John Mills Kendrick is named Episcopal Bishop of Arizona, New Mexico, and Texas west of the Pecos. (B)

MAR. 2. Atlantic & Pacific train held up at Canyon Diablo and express box taken. (39)

APRIL 9. Lewis Wolfley is appointed governor. (56)

APRIL 12. Governor Wolfley is burned in effigy at Flagstaff for vetoing a bill creating Coconino County. (70)

APRIL 30. All Arizona joins in celebrating centennial of the inauguration of George Washington as President. (74)

MAY 11. Band of masked men ambush Maj. J. W. Wham and military escort carrying $26,000 army payroll to Fort Thomas. Eight soldiers wounded. Eight cattlemen arrested. (B–C)

JULY 23. Prescott merchants boycott Prescott and Arizona railway in protest against high freight rates. (70)

SEPT. 14. Postmaster General informs Arizona that federal government will pay a reward of $1000 for arrest and conviction of every person convicted in U. S. Court of armed attack on stagecoach or railway car carrying government mail. (70)

NOV. 2. Sheriff Glenn Reynolds and Deputy Sheriff W. A. Holmes of Globe are killed by the Apache Kid and seven other Apaches whom they are escorting to penitentiary. (74)

NOV. 20. Pearl Hart, notorious female bandit is tried in Florence for holdup, convicted and sentenced to five years in prison. (39)

DEC. 14. Tucson jury acquits all the defendants in the Wham robbery case. (74)

DEC. 30. Prescott constable tries to serve warrant on horse thief. Thief goes for his gun and constable kills him. (70)

Property valuation of Arizona set at $27,057,460. (39)

Total major minerals production in Arizona, $6,574,135. (22)

Total number of cattle in Arizona, 980,000; value, $14,750,000. (50)

1890 JAN. 2. Phoenix reports $488,000 in new buildings since it acquired the state capital in January of 1889. (69)

JAN. 25. Standard Pullman car service is established between Maricopa and Phoenix. (74)

JAN. 26. Two Tucson teachers, discharged for enforcing discipline with corporal punishment, are returned to their positions by the Territorial Supreme Court and collect four months' back pay. (60)

JAN. 28. Epidemic of "spotted fever"sweeps towns along the Gila River. (60)

JAN. 31. Empire Ranch starts driving 1,000 head of cattle to California to escape excessive freight rates. (60)

FEB. 2. Tombstone prospector reports with much satisfaction that no Indian is known to have recovered from an attack of influenza, which at the time is of epidemic proportions. (60)

FEB. 9. Arizona Pioneers' Society files strong protest against General Crook's policy of moving Apache prisoners from Alabama to Indian Territory. (60)

FEB. 15. Five masked robbers hold up Southern Pacific passenger train at Fairbank. Jeff Milton, express messenger, is wounded but fights off robbers and mortally wounds "Three Finger Jack." (74)

FEB. 16. Midnight battle develops at Red Rock station when band of tramps attempts to capture Southern Pacific fast freight. (74)

FEB. 21. Four-day rain sends Granite Creek on rampage and all trains are halted for bridge and track repairs. (70)

FEB. 22. Weakened by rains and flood waters Walnut Grove Dam on the Hassayampa River collapses causing the loss of 50 lives and carrying destruction as far south as Wickenburg. (60)

FEB. 28. J. A. P. Reavis of Peralta Grant fame files notice at Phoenix of his intention of appropriating all Gila River water below Mineral Creek. (74)

MAR. 16. Tucson receives $25,000 from Andrew Carnegie for a library. (74)

MAR. 28. Supreme Court declares acts passed by Governor Zulick's holdovers in legislature are invalid. (70)

MAR. 30. Fire wipes out block of business buildings in Flagstaff. (70)

JUNE 7. Mine fuel tanks at Pearce explode, destroying 50-stamp mill and setting section of the town ablaze. (74)

JUNE 30. N. O. Murphy, acting governor, reports to the Secretary of the Interior that all property valuations in Arizona should be doubled. (A)

JULY 16. Warren Earp, youngest and last of the brothers in Cochise County, starts a fight in Willcox saloon and is killed. (74)

JULY 14. Fire originating in miner's shack on "Whiskey Row," all but wipes out Prescott. Bank, hotels, stores, newspaper plants and scores of dwellings are destroyed. (74)

JULY 24. Gasoline stove explodes in Yuma, and eight business buildings are destroyed. (74)

AUG. 12. Prof. Frank A. Gully is made first faculty member of the University of Airzona by Board of Regents. (36)

AUG. 14. Citizens turn out to chase a horse thief who has been raiding Prescott pastures and bring their man back dead. (70)

SEPT. 12. Democratic Territorial Convention meets in Phoenix and police are called to quell floor battle for control. (74)

OCT. 4. John N. Irwin appointed governor upon removal of Wolfley. (56)

OCT. 11. Yuma prison enters into contract to supply prison labor for the making of hemp rope. (74)

OCT. 18. Bowie and Solomon Stage is robbed by Mexican bandits. (74)

OCT. 20. Gen. Nelson A. Miles recommends that abandoned military posts in Arizona be used for Indian reservations or schools. (74)

NOV. 10. Territorial Board of Equalization assesses Arizona property at $28,050,234.78. (74)

NOV. 11. *Arizona Republican* first published in Phoenix. (35)

DEC. 31. U. S. Census reports Arizona population as 88,243; a gain of 118.2 per cent. (49) U. S. Census credits Arizona with 1,526 farms and 104,128 acres of improved land. Total value with buildings $7,-222,230. Total value all livestock $13,924,000. Total number of livestock, 984,000. Estimated value of farm crops for 1889, $2,472,348. (49–50)

Average daily attendance in public schools, 4,702. (13)

Total major minerals production in Arizona, $7,478,283. (22)

1891 JAN. 4. Government decides to establish an Indian School near Phoenix. (68)

JAN. 16. Phoenix makes plans to open a free public reading room. (60)

JAN. 16. Herd of 2,000 steers passes Tucson as cattlemen continue drives to coast to avoid railroad charge of $7 a head. (60)

JAN. 19. Acting Gov. N. O. Murphy meets with the Sixteenth Territorial Legislature in Phoenix. He tells the members that while the value of property is increasing, the people are paying less in taxes because property owners conceal their holdings. Coconino County is created by dividing Yavapai County. (31)

JAN. 21. After years of agitation, contract is finally let for a wagon road between Globe and Florence. (60)

FEB. 8. T. A. Gulley, director of University's experiment station, proves practicability of pumping underground water for irrigation on UA campus. (36)

FEB. 9. Arizona Press Association is organized at Tucson. (60)

FEB. 11. President Benjamin Harrsion approves Act of Congress providing a fourth supreme court judge for Territory. (60)

FEB. 12. Territorial Supreme Court rules that Arizona has right to tax railroad property on Indian reservation lands. (60)

FEB. 18–24. Gila, Little Colorado, Salt, and Colorado rivers go wild, damaging Prescott, Globe, Holbrook, Solomonville, Clifton and San Carlos. Railroad tracks ripped out, homes destroyed. (60)

FEB. 19. Phoenix suffers heavy losses as Salt River "rolls" in its biggest flood in recorded history. (61)

FEB. 28. City of Yuma is practically wiped out as levee breaks on the Gila. Colorado rises 33 feet in 20 minutes. Two hundred and sixty-five buildings are destroyed as water reaches depth of nine feet in city streets. Inhabitants flee to high mesa. Twenty-four miles of Southern Pacific track are swept away. (60–62)

MAR. 17. Women's Suffrage is defeated in upper house of the legislature by a tie vote. (60)

MAR. 19. Territorial legislature authorizes funds for Arizona participation in the World's Columbian Exposition of 1893. (74)

MAR. 25. Arizona Pioneers Historical Society files articles of incorporation with Secretary of the Territory. (60)

APRIL 21. President William H. Harrison tours Arizona by special train. (60)

JUNE 2. Arizona holds constitutional convention providing for statehood. People accept it but Congress is not impressed. (68)

JUNE 7. Yuma commences pumping water from the Colorado for irrigation project. (61)

JUNE 11. Geronimo, notorious Mexican road agent, killed in Rincon Mountains by sheriff's posse. (60)

JULY 1. Southern Pacific trainmen discover Colorado River has burst its banks near Pilot Knob and flooded immense marshes. (60)

JULY 2. Fire wipes out the town of Williams. (70)

JULY 8. Yuma reports that Colorado has cut a channel into the Salton Sea and is pouring vast quantities of water into that body. (60)

JULY 21. Secretary of the Interior rejects plea of California citizen that Southern Pacific be enjoined from attempting to close the break through which Colorado River is flowing into the Salton Sea. (74)

AUG. 6. Earthquake, followed by tidal wave, does great damage to Cocopah Indian villages and lands on lower Colorado. (60)

SEPT. 6. Tucson sprinkles 17,000 gallons of water daily on downtown streets to lay the dust. (61)

SEPT. 7. Enthusiastic citizens stage what they call a "Constitutional Convention" in Phoenix. (61)

SEPT. 24. Dr. J. C. Handy, former chancellor of the University of Arizona provokes battle at Pennington and Church streets, Tucson, with Att. Francis J. Heney and is fatally wounded in struggle. (74)

OCT. 1. University of Arizona opens its doors. (36)

OCT. 2. Citizens of Phoenix frame a state constitution providing for free silver and federal and state aid for railroads. (2–56)

NOV. 14. Governor Murphy makes annual report to Washington and recommends that all Indian reservations with possible exception of Navajo lands be turned over to the whites for sale and settlement. (70)

Total major minerals production in Arizona, $7,543,980. (22)

Total number of cattle in Arizona, 963,000; value, $14,565,000. (50)

1892 JAN. 10. Florence *Tribune* appears. (35)

JAN. 12. Man, woman, and child murdered near Solomonville and wagon plundered. Killers escape. (60)

JAN. 16. Supreme Court of Arizona rules that a squatter has no ownership rights in a building built on another's land and cannot collect damages if it is destroyed. (60)

JAN. 20. Fire destroys historical quarters at old Fort Yuma. (60)

JAN. 20. First issue of Tucson *Enterprise* appears and enrages lawyers by calling the Pima County bar "infamous." (60)

JAN. 23. Tombstone makes another effort to recover silver deposits and installs diamond drill in the Lucky Cuss mine. (60)

FEB. 23. Pima recorder announces that 33,000 mining claims have been filed in county. (74)

FEB. 24. Yuma reports having been shaken by earthquake. (60)

MAY 11. Nathan O. Murphy is appointed governor. Murphy served as tenth and fourteenth Territorial governor. (56)

MAY 19. Stagecoach line established between Flagstaff and Grand Canyon. (68)

MAY 25. Arizona Medical Association is organized in Phoenix. Incorporated June 16, 1950. (10)

JUNE 22. Casa Grande ruins are declared a national reservation by President Benjamin Harrison. (33)

JULY 3. Police officer armed with pistol and Mexican with knife duel to the death on Meyer Street in Tucson. (60)

JULY 7. Mexican band is declared a public nuisance by Phoenix city council because it practices all day and plays all night. (68)

JULY 13. Nogales citizens hold mass meeting to denounce claimants to their lands and burn two of them in effigy. (60)

JULY 22. U. S. Land commissioners notify Arizona settlers who have held adverse possession of lands for 20 years that they have no title unless land was not originally confirmed by a grant. (70)

JULY 22. Tucson suffers a shortage of domestic help who do not find monthly wage of $10 or $15 attractive. (60)

Total major minerals production in Arizona, $6,539,440. (22)

Total number of cattle in Arizona, 943,000; value, $14,316,000. (50)

1893 JAN. 3. Ground is broken for Arizona-New Mexico-Oklahoma building at Chicago World's Fair. (74)

JAN. 17. Phoenix lets a contract for 25 electric street lights. (68)

FEB. 8. Federal postal department begins installation of neighborhood postboxes. (74)

FEB. 13. Governor Murphy meets with Seventeenth Territorial Legislature. Says the bonded indebtedness of the Territory and its counties is $2,956,000; that the Territory exceeded its income by $78,000 in 1892 and that the assessed valuation of the Territory is only $28 million. Murphy favors exempting new railroads from taxation. (31)

FEB. 20. Congressional Act of this date restores a portion of the White Mountain Reservation to public domain (27 Stat., 469-470, c. 147). (32)

MAR. 6. Supervisors of Maricopa County decide to confer with supervisors of Pinal County over methods of fighting the Peralta Grant. (74)

APRIL 5. President Grover Cleveland appoints L. C. Hughes governor of Arizona. (74)

APRIL 8. Governor commutes sentences of two editors of Arizona papers convicted of criminal libel from five days in penitentiary to five days in Pima County jail. (74)

APRIL 20. Tucson circulates petition against proposed Papago reservation. (74)

JULY 3. Rumor that the "Apache Kid" is in town brings Tempe citizens out armed with every pistol, rifle, and shotgun in city. (61)

JULY 9. Phoenicians suffer from gold fever and rush to the Superstition Mountains to stake claims. (61)

JULY 11. Yuma reports it is shipping carload of melons a day to Pacific Coast. (61)

JULY 13. Hayden's mill on the Gila reports that Pima Indians are delivering from 6,000 to 10,000 pounds of wheat daily. (61)

JULY 22. Nogales is incorporated. Its history goes back to the fifties. (34)

AUG. 16. Bank closes in Phoenix and some businesses fail as national financial panic is felt in Arizona. (74)

SEPT. 12. Cattlemen and farmers of Cochise and Graham counties are warned to go armed at all times because of rumors that Apache Kid is lurking in the mountains. (61)

SEPT. 19. Governor Hughes makes strong appeal for statehood in his annual report to Secretary of the Interior. (61)

SEPT. 23. Editor G. M. Russell of the Gila Bend *Arizonan* and a newsdealer engage in a rifle and pistol duel on main street. No casualties. (61)

SEPT. 26. Sheriff of Coconino and posse kill two Phoenix horse thieves on the Verde River. (61)

SEPT. 27. Papago Indians are accused of slaughtering two prospectors and a boy at Gila City. (61)

OCT. 3. Governor Hughes issues proclamation urging Arizonans to support Second International Irrigation Congress on Arid Lands meeting in Los Angeles. University sends president and two scientists. (61)

OCT. 18. Hundreds of unemployed men in California move east along the railroad tracks. Tucson police patrol tracks, give each man a loaf of bread and order him to move on. (74)

OCT. 20. Federal government gives state penitentiary at Yuma 2,000 acres of land on which convicts are expected to work farms. (61)

NOV. 1. Arizona suffers as Sherman Silver Purchase Act is repealed and silver drops from $1.25 to as low as 25 cents an ounce. Many Arizona mines close. (44)

NOV. 3. John O. Dunbar, editor of the *Phoenix Gazette* and his attorney, Judge W. H. Barnes are sentenced to a ten-day term in the Tucson jail for contempt of court. They spend one night behind bars, appeal and are cleared. (74)

NOV. 16. Order of the Grand Commandery of Knights Templar is organized in Phoenix. (16)

Plagued by a long drouth and the effects of overgrazing the ranges, cattlemen of Southern Arizona experience a 50 to 75 per cent mortality among their stock and ship 200,000 head of all classes out of the state. (A. Bulletin No. 20)

Total major minerals production in Arizona, $8,215,551. (22)

Total number of cattle in Arizona, 940,000; value, $10,616,000. (50)

1894 JAN. 6. Prescott chief of police and constable duel over custody of a prisoner. (68)

JAN. 17. Citizens of Yuma agitate for wooden sidewalks. (68)

JAN. 20. Fred G. Hughes issues a challenge in the Phoenix *Citizen* offering ten dollars to anyone who "can name a bigger liar than Gov. L. C. Hughes." (74)

JAN. 21. Government closes post office at Silver King as mining ceases and once rich camp dies. (68)

MAR. 7. Temple hotel at Tempe destroyed by fire. (68)

MAR. 11. Territorial Livestock Commission moves to wipe out epidemic of glanders by killing horses and burning carcasses. (68)

MAR. 30. Court of private land claims voids Spanish land grants along the border. Nogales, Huachuca, and Tombstone hold all night celebration with bonfires and salutes. (60–68)

APRIL 17. Business district of Jerome, largest mining camp in Arizona, is destroyed by fire. (60)

MAY 22. Dr. A. E. Douglass selects site at Flagstaff for Lowell Observatory. (39)

MAY 26. City of Flagstaff incorporated. (Letter)

JUNE 9. Flourishing town of Globe destroyed by fire. (68)

JUNE 23. Gila Bend brings in artesian well and town celebrates. (60)

JULY 8. Phoenix is without mail for eleven days due to nationwide railroad strike. (68)

SEPT. 1. Cloudburst in Graham Mountains sweeps Willcox with two feet of water. Adobe buildings crumble. (60)

SEPT. 30. Eastbound express of Southern Pacific held up at Maricopa by train robbers. (68)

Total major minerals production in Arizona, $7,287,416. (22)

Total number of cattle in Arizona, 900,000; value, $8,834,000. (50)

City of Tempe, Maricopa County, incorporates. (34)

City of Flagstaff, Coconino County, incorporated. (34)

1895 JAN. 21. Gov. L. C. Hughes takes over on last day of the Seventeenth Legislature and meets the Eighteenth Territorial Legislature in Phoenix. He declares that taxable property is assessed far below its value. Navajo County is created from the western half of Apache County. (31)

JAN. 26. Prescott is isolated for a week by winter floods. (68)

JAN. 30. Train robbers hold up Southern Pacific westbound passenger train, blast the strong box and blow Mexican silver pesos across the desert. (68)

MAR. 12. Thousands celebrate arrival of first Santa Fe train in Phoenix. (68)

MAR. 31. Observatory at Flagstaff is abandoned. Reopens later. (68)

APRIL 27. Indian tribes at San Carlos Reservation threaten war if railroad persists in crossing their lands without paying for a right of way. They got nothing and did nothing. (68)

JUNE 19. J. O. Dunbar, editor of the *Phoenix Gazette,* who called the governor, Territorial secretary, attorney general and marshal "assassins, looters, hoodoos, patronage peddlers and land grant sharks" is tried and convicted of libel in Tucson and is fined $1,000. (68)

JUNE 26. Famous Peralta-Reavis claims to 12,750,000 acres of land in Arizona and New Mexico are declared fraudulent by U.S. Court at Santa Fe. Reavis later convicted of perjury and sentenced to two years in penitentiary. (68)

JULY 11. Gasoline stove explodes in a Williams tailor shop and two blocks of flimsy wooden stores are destroyed. (68)

JULY 14. Indians of the Pima villages go to court and charge Arizona Canal Company with stealing water guaranteed Pimas under contract. (68)

AUG. 4. Phoenix firm opens first packing house built in Arizona. (68)

AUG. 30. Dr. Theodore Comstock, first president of University of Arizona, resigns. (60)

SEPT. 26. Maricopa farmers meet, form Co-operative and Protective Assn., and adopt a constitution. (68)

OCT. 5. Gila River rolls and tears out section of railroad bridge near Maricopa. (60)

OCT. 11. Stagecoach robber who held up Casa Grande stage twice, confesses and is sentenced to life imprisonment at Yuma. (60)

OCT. 19. Settlement at Williams is incorporated. (34)

Total major minerals production in Arizona, $7,533,532. (22)

Total number of cattle in Arizona, 880,000; value, $9,126,000. (50)

1896 JAN. 28. Hobo gang resists officers at Benson. Two hoboes die and one officer is wounded in gun battle. (60)

FEB. 24. Tucson businessmen organize a Chamber of Commerce. (60)

MAR. 30. Governor Hughes is removed from office due to disagreement with Congress over public lands, and President Grover Cleveland appoints Benjamin J. Franklin to fill the vacancy. (31–39–56)

APRIL 25. Plague sweeps hog farms in Salt River Valley. Eight thousand hogs die in three months. (60)

APRIL 27. First passenger elevator in Arizona placed in service in Phoenix. (60)

MAY 6. *Bisbee Daily Review* established. (52)

JUNE 7. A Congressional Act provides that the portion of the White Mountain Reservation south of the Salt or Black River is to compose the San Carlos Reservation. The portion north of the Salt or Black River is to be known as the Fort Apache Reservation. (32)

JUNE 19. Maricopa beekeepers ship first two of 13 carloads of honey to the East. (60)

JUNE 30. Territorial Supreme Court rules that governor has power to remove any Territorial official. (60)

JUNE 30. James Addison Reavis is found guilty of fraud in Federal Court and sentenced to two years in the penitentiary. (45)

AUG. 6. Five bank robbers attempt to hold up International Bank in Nogales. Cashier drives them off with rifle. They escape. (60)

AUG. 12. Citizens arm and Fort Huachuca rushes troops to Nogales where band of Yaqui Indians raid border customs office in attempt to capture arms and ammunition. (60)

AUG. 26. Pima County cattlemen set up permanent organization to protect cattle from constant depredations of renegade Papagos. (60)

SEPT. 25. Tucson school board decides it cannot afford to open high school for six students. (60)

OCT. 1. Flash floods caused by two cloudbursts in Whetstone mountains sweep Benson. Two mothers and four children die. (60)

Total major minerals production in Arizona, $11,851,912. (22)

Total number of cattle in Arizona, 865,000; value, $10,560,000. (50)

1897 JAN. 5. Tucson city council holds first meeting of the year and mayor reveals that city has been victim of diphtheria epidemic. Attributes disease to "garbage and filth" accumulating on streets and about homes. Pleads for sewers and more water. (74)

JAN. 18. Gov. B. J. Franklin is ill when the Nineteenth Territorial Legislature convenes but delivers his message on Jan. 28. He scores corporations for failure to "make a proper return for the special privileges granted them." Legislators introduced 320 bills, 88 of which were enacted into laws. One provided $19,800 for the completion of the Normal School building at Tempe. (31)

JAN. 27. Settlement at Pearce in midst of mining and building boom. Huge stamp mill ordered and deserted homes brought in from Tombstone. (74)

JAN. 30. Woman's suffrage bill is introduced in the legislature as usual and this time is referred to the committee on mines and mining. (60)

FEB. 9. Legislature passes law defining a legal newspaper as a journal which has been published within a county for 52 successive weeks and has a circulation of 200 or more. (60)

FEB. 23. Prescott makes determined effort to get the penitentiary from Yuma but move is beaten in the upper house of the legislature. (60)

FEB. 24. Tucson, Benson, Tombstone, and Pantano report brilliant meteor passing overhead at low altitude. (60)

APRIL 10. Rumors of rich gold strikes in the Yuma area fill the town with miners and promoters. (60)

MAY 4. Tucson chief of police asks city council for horse and saddle or buggy for patrolling the town. Request refused because it will cost $12 a month to feed horse. (60)

MAY 19. Myron H. McCord is named Territorial governor. (60)

JULY 3. James C. Burnett kills William Green whom he charged with having blown up dam and caused death of a Burnett child. Jury acquits Burnett. (60)

JULY 18. Appointment of Myron H. McCord as Territorial governor is confirmed after bitter fight against him by Arizona Bank. (74)

OCT. 14. President of the Arizona Pioneers Historical Society is charged with stealing $2,000 of the Society's funds and flees to Guaymas. (60)

NOV. 11. Tucson's pride, a new opera house, is opened. (60)

NOV. 11. Four miners stage gun battle over claims near Prescott. Two die, two are wounded. (60)

Total major minerals production in Arizona, $14,180,776. (22)

Total number of cattle in Arizona, 850,000; value, $13,202,000. (50)

1898 JAN. 4. Phoenix dedicates first high school building. (61)

JAN. 5. Mayor H. Buehman delivers annual message to Tucson city council and deplores fact that "our boys and girls are growing up in an atmosphere which is far from bracing." (60)

FEB. 4. Gov. M. H. McCord formally opens Tempe Normal's new building. (61)

FEB. 21. Prescott leads state by offering to raise a regiment of cavalry composed of Arizona cowboys for the war which it feels will follow the sinking of the Battleship Maine. (60)

MAR. 1. Phoenix citizens hold mass meeting and petition Congress to recognize independence of Cuba. (61)

MAR. 8. Citizens of Tucson hold meeting and urge Washington to recognize independence of Cuba. (60)

MAR. 10. General Land Office rules that cutting of mesquite trees on government lands is illegal; reverses decision one week later declaring mesquite is not wood. (61)

MAR. 13. Arizona Press Association calls for a storage reservoir at the Buttes in Pinal County to aid 4,000 Indians whose crops are dying because they have been robbed of their Gila River water by settlers on the Gila (Pima Indian) Reservation. (60)

APRIL 5. Mining Camp at Congress wiped out by fire. Two deaths; property loss $50,000. (61)

APRIL 15. War Department begins to move troops stationed in Arizona to the coast. (60)

APRIL 27. Arizonans enlist in Rough Riders for service in the Spanish American war. (1)

APRIL 29. First contingent of Arizona volunteers heads for Cuba via El Paso. (61)

MAY 2. All Arizona goes mad with enthusiasm as Dewey is victorious over Spanish fleet in Manila Bay. (61)

MAY 3. Governor McCord issues proclamation informing citizens that Arizona quota for military duty in Spanish-American War has been exceeded by fifteen per cent and no more volunteers will be accepted. (60)

MAY 4. Arizona's last group of men destined for Roosevelt's Rough Riders leave Fort Whipple for San Antonio. (61)

MAY 16. Arizona barbers raise the price of a shave to 25 cents. (60)

MAY 19. War department authorizes Arizona to recruit 100 volunteers who can shoot and ride, for duty in the Philippines. (61)

MAY 24. Governor McCord files claim to 3,000 acres in the Algodones grant in the name of the University of Arizona. (61)

JUNE 3. James Parker, notorious desperado, dies on Prescott gallows for murder. (61)

JUNE 28. Governor McCord authorized to raise a second regiment of troops for war in Cuba. (61)

JULY 15. Right Reverend Archbishop Salpointe dies in Phoenix, and Arizona mourns passing of great churchman and citizen. (60)

JULY 19. Governor McCord resigns to lead regiment in Cuba, and N. O. Murphy is appointed governor by President McKinley. (60)

AUG. 14. Violent storm sweeps Gila Bend, demolishes school house, blows drug store off foundations, wrecks Southern Pacific roundhouse and overturns freight cars. (60)

AUG. 15. Locomotive boiler explodes in Prescott destroying roundhouse and killing two men. (61)

SEPT. 2. Colonel McCord's new regiment is mustered out of service. (61)

SEPT. 6. Hurricane unroofs homes at Casa Grande. One death. (60)

SEPT. 11. Fire destroys Jerome. Three die; 1500 are homeless. (61)

SEPT. 14. First carload of almonds from Salt River Valley leaves for Chicago. (60)

Total major minerals production in Arizona, $17,743,358. (22)

Total number of cattle in Arizona, 850,000; value, $14,594,000. (50)

1899 JAN. 16. Governor Murphy meets with Twentieth Territorial Legislature. Fifteen year tax exemption granted for water development and 10-year exemption for railroads. Normal school established at Flagstaff. Pima County is carved up again and southeastern corner is named Santa Cruz County. (31)

MAR. 8. Town of Jerome incorporated. (Letter)

MAR. 15. Governor Murphy signs bill creating Santa Cruz County from lands cut from Pima. (57)

APRIL 5. Town of Thatcher is incorporated.

APRIL 24. Santa Cruz board of supervisors establishes twelve school districts. (57)

JULY 28. Tucson businessmen subscribe $1,100 towards cost of a wagon road to Globe. Shortest road at the time takes 48 hours. (74)

SEPT. 9. Southern Pacific train held up at Cochise and $10,000 taken. Two constables are caught and convicted. (39)

SEPT. 11. First school term of Northern Arizona Normal School (Flagstaff) opens. (44)

DEC. 10. Fritzie Scheff, noted light opera star is annoyed when water in private tub aboard her Southern Pacific special train splashes her bathroom. She stops the train in Stein's Pass until her toilet is completed. (74)

DEC. 14. Regents authorize first bond issue for University of Arizona. (5)

DEC. 15. Gila Valley Bank founded at Solomon. Doors opened Jan. 16, 1900. First of the Valley National Banks. (12)

Property valuation of Arizona is set at $32,473,540. (39)

Total major minerals production in Arizona, $26,569,391. (22)

Total number of cattle in Arizona, 850,000; value, $14,330,000. (50)

1900 JAN. 4. City of Winslow is incorporated.

JAN. 8. An executive order enlarges the areas of the Hopi and Navajo reservations. (32)

MAY 8. President William McKinley spends a day in Phoenix, makes a whistle stop in Tucson, fails to mention statehood for Arizona. (39)

MAY 17. A. & N. M. freight train crashes through bridge near Clifton. Three killed, nine injured. (74)

NOV. 18. Two Haldeman brothers legally hanged in Tombstone for killing two peace officers. (78)

DEC. 25. Wild gun battle breaks out at Silver Springs in saloon tent when gunman tries to hold up bartender. Thirty shots fired. One killed, one wounded. (74)

DEC. 27. Lone bandit holds up Hot Springs stage. (74)

DEC. 31. Total major metals production in Arizona, $26,021,049. (22)

U. S. census reports Arizona population as 122,931, a gain of 39.3 percent. (49)

Total number of all cattle in Arizona, 848,000; value, $14,368,000. (50)

Town of Wickenburg incorporated in Maricopa County. (34)

1901 JAN. 6. Yuma rejoices over wire from Washington announcing that federal government will open the 35,000 acre Algodones land grant for settlement. (74)

JAN. 14. Work begins on long distance telephone line between Arizona and Guaymas. (74)

JAN. 21. Twenty-first Territorial Legislature convenes in the new capitol building in Phoenix, writes a new civil code and authorizes Governor Murphy to form a small company of Arizona Rangers. Another attempt to write a "bullion tax" on mines fails. (1)

JAN. 22. Wool growers of Coconino County hold meeting and indignantly protest Department of Agriculture ruling barring sheep from Federal forest reserves. Delegation is appointed to carry protest to President William McKinley. (68)

FEB. 24. New state capitol is dedicated with aid of three punch bowls. (36)

MAR. 2. A Congressional Act restores a portion of the "White Mountain" Reservation to public domain (31 Stat. 952, c. 810). (32)

MAR. 11. E. B. Gage, Frank Murphy, and others reorganize Tombstone mining companies and prepare to pump out the flooded mines. (74)

MAR. 18. Territorial Legislature adopts the Saguaro blossom as the official Arizona flower. (39)

MAR. 25. Prospectors find gold four miles from Wickenburg and there is a rush of placer miners to the Hassayampa. (68)

APRIL 1. Board of National Missions approves building of Ganado Mission for the Navajos. It becomes largest Indian church hospital in Arizona. Forty years in the desert. (B)

APRIL 20. Arizona veterans of the war in the Philippines are discharged and return home. (68)

APRIL 27. Mayor Shumaker of Tucson threatens to jail ministers, priests, and justices of the peace who fail to report marriages, as well as doctors and nurses who do not report births and deaths for the public records. (68)

JUNE 17. President Theodore Roosevelt signs Reclamation Act which assures Arizona of a great future. (1)

JULY 3. Fire destroys the tenderloin district in Globe. (74)

JULY 9. City of Williams is incorporated. (Letter)

JULY 21. Burton W. Mossman named captain and authorized to raise company of ten or twelve Arizona Rangers to hunt cattle rustlers and other criminals. (74)

AUG. 2. Director of U. S. Census reports that Arizona has 5,800 farms covering 1,935,287 acres of which 254,521 acres are improved land. (74)

SEPT. 27. U. S. District Attorney charges scandalous conditions prevail at Nogales Customs office where federal officials are engaged in smuggling Chinese into Arizona from Mexico. (74)

OCT. 26. Arizonans hold statehood conference in Phoenix and appoint committee of prominent men to visit Washington and urge statehood on congressmen and senators. (74)

Total major metals production in Arizona, $27,958,338. (22)

Total number of all cattle in Arizona, 850,000; value, $14,577,000. (50)

City of Safford, Graham County, incorporates. (34)

1902 JAN. 1. Experimental plantings of Egyptian cotton in the Salt River Valley develop the finest cotton yet grown in the U.S. (74)

JAN. 3. U. S. quarantine against Sonora cattle is disastrous blow to Arizona commission men. (74)

JAN. 4. Greene Consolidated Copper Co., completes railroad between Cananea and Naco. (67)

JAN. 9. Town of Bisbee is incorporated. March 15 the mayor and common council change the official name to City of Bisbee. (34)

JAN. 28. Senator Eugene S. Ives accuses Gov. Nathan O. Murphy of malfeasance and files protest with President Theodore Roosevelt. (74)

FEB. 22. Rivals quarrel over ownership of the *Phoenix Gazette* and publish two papers. (74)

MAR. 8. Construction of Territorial Reform School begins at Benson. (74)

APRIL 11. British begin buying hundreds of horses in Arizona for use of the army in Boer War. (60)

APRIL 12. Village of Yuma incorporated as a town. Became a city in 1914.

MAY 6. President Theodore Roosevelt makes first of four trips to Arizona. He calls the Grand Canyon, "Awful." (39)

MAY 7. Governor Murphy resigns and President Roosevelt appoints Alexander O. Brodie, his comrade of Rough Rider days, to fill vacancy on July 1. (60)

MAR. 13. *Douglas Dispatch* established. (35)

JUNE 22. Government announces it will cut off beef rations of Apaches July 1, and Indians shoot up agency at San Carlos. (70)

JUNE 24. Charles D. Poston, "Father of Arizona," dies in Phoenix in poverty. (23)

JULY 14. War Department appropriates $120,000 for re-activation of Fort Whipple. (70)

SEPT. 15. A portion of Camp McDowell, abandoned by the military, is set aside by an executive order as the Fort McDowell Reservation for Mohave-Apache Indians. (32)

NOV. 22. Consolidated Mines Co., reopens Tombstone silver mines. (78)

DEC. 22. Certain portions of the Fort Apache Reservation are restored to public domain by an executive order. (32)

Total major minerals production in Arizona, $20,497,544. (22)

Total number of cattle in Arizona, 855,000; value, $14,571,000. (50)

1903 JAN. 8. Tucson Board of Trade petitions Washington to safeguard Arizona against so-called "plague" in Mexico. (70)

JAN. 18. The day of the fast gun has not yet passed in Prescott where a bartender shoots down a customer in an argument over a hat. (70)

JAN. 19. Twenty-second Territorial Legislature meets with Gov. Alexander O. Brodie; approves eight-hour day for underground miners, doubles the size of the Arizona Rangers command, exempts sugar beet factories from taxes for nine years, requires physicians to have a license before practicing and orders every school to buy an American flag. (31)

JAN. 21. Salt River Valley Water Users files articles of incorporation. (B)

JAN. 22. Southern Pacific east and west bound passenger trains crash head on near Vail's Station. Twenty-two die and 45 are injured in crash and flaming wreckage. (60)

FEB. 2. Robbers kill two at lonely Goddard Station. (70)

FEB. 4. Salt River Valley Water Users Association is organized. (1)

FEB. 5. Territorial Legislature wires Congressional Delegate Mark Smith that it is unalterably opposed to the bill which would admit Arizona and New Mexico to the Union as one State. (70)

MAR. 9. Four convicts escape from Territorial Prison at Yuma, flee down the Colorado and seize a yacht but go aground on a sandbar and are caught in the desert. (70)

MAR. 13. Eight-hour day for underground miners is signed into law by Governor Brodie. (60)

MAR. 14. Salt River Valley ranchers ship 1,300,000 pounds of wool. (60)

MAR. 18. Legislature passes Women's Suffrage bill. Governor Brodie kills it with veto the following day. (60)

MAY 14. Salt River Valley project is authorized by the Bureau of Reclamation. (56)

JUNE 6. Governor Brodie orders Arizona Rangers to Morenci and Clifton where miners are striking for ten hours pay for eight hours work. (60)

JUNE 9. Pumps are shut down as Tombstone miners strike. Water rises in the mines. (60)

JUNE 10. Eleven drown at Clifton as cloudburst sweeps town. (60)

JUNE 11. Armed strikers seize mill at Morenci. President Roosevelt orders detachments from Fort Grant and Fort Huachuca to scene. Operators and miners compromise; nine hours pay for eight hours work. (60)

JULY 13. Fifty Fort Grant soldiers stage fight. One killed, two wounded. (60)

JULY 16. Heavy rainfall strikes Ash Fork and sidewalks float down the streets in two feet of water. (70)

JULY 17. Subscription books of Water Users Association close at Phoenix. Land owners give government lien on 195,000 acres of land to insure building of Roosevelt Dam. (60)

JULY 21. Heavy rainstorm between Dragoon Mountains and Tombstone, washes out six El Paso and Southwestern railroad bridges and floods Fairbank with six feet of water. (70)

JULY 31. *Journal-Miner* at Prescott announces that hanging of two murderers "was from a professional or official standpoint" a perfect success. (70)

AUG. 21. Cloudburst in San Francisco Mountains sends eight-foot wall of water over Flagstaff farms. (60)

OCT. 3. Methodist Episcopal Church is organized in Douglas. (Graphic)

OCT. 5. U. S. Department of Interior authorizes construction of Tonto Basin (Roosevelt) Dam. It is first great irrigation enterprise attempted by federal government. (39)

NOV. 13. Arizona Bankers' Association is organized at Phoenix. (70)

DEC. 15. Tombstone sets another record when Billy Stiles and Burt Alvord break out of jail for the second time and take 11 other prisoners with them. (78)

DEC. 28. Arizona closes the year with a fire in the State Capitol. (60)

Total major metals production in Arizona, $26,539,859. (22)

Total number of cattle in Arizona, 900,000; value, $15,923,000. (50)

1904 JAN. 5. Arizona Cattle Growers Association organizes at Phoenix. One hundred cattlemen in attendance. (53)

JAN. 8. H. J. Allen, financial manager of Senator Clark's United Verde mine, creates wide sensation by committing suicide. Special funeral train filled with friends carries body from Jerome to Prescott. (70)

JAN. 14. International Bank of Nogales fails. Collapse is heavy blow to economy of the area. (74)

JAN. 20. Annual winter invasion of "tramps" keeps Tucson police busy following up reports of holdups and burglaries. (74)

FEB. 1. Santa Rita Hotel, largest hostelry in Arizona, is opened at midnight in Tucson. (74)

FEB. 8. Three attempts at street holdups of pedestrians show that Prescott is still a tough town. (60)

FEB. 19. Burt Alvord, notorious Cochise County outlaw, is wounded and captured near Naco. (74)

FEB. 20. State newspapers quarrel over action of Board of Regents of the University which secretly sells machinery to its chancellor. Governor Brodie ignores the matter. (74)

MAR. 12. Territorial Supreme Court rules that Supervisors of Yavapai County have no authority to lower taxes of the United Verde Copper Co. (70)

APRIL 3. Leaking gas main explodes in Prescott saloon and gambling house, injuring four. (70)

APRIL 21. Edward Tewksbury, last survivor of the Graham-Tewksbury feud, dies in bed. (60)

MAY 4. Prescott auto owners try tour to Tucson but are hindered by deep sand and high centers. (70)

JUNE 9. Fire of incendiary origin in Nogales destroys Southern Pacific station, U. S. Customs, Wells Fargo depot and freight cars. (60)

JUNE 12. U. S. Department of Agriculture experiments with cotton in Yuma Valley. Reports noteworthy success. (60)

AUG. 3. Heavy rains fall at Kingman. Needles and Ashfork. Traffic halts on Santa Fe, which continues transcontinental service by routing trains from Deming to Tucson. (60)

AUG. 14. Tucson police begin series of raids designed to close city's opium dens. (60)

AUG. 19. Two-inch rain falls at Globe in one hour. Six persons drown, 20 business places are destroyed, and numerous railroad bridges are washed away. (60)

AUG. 31. Phoenix public schools enter the only Arizona exhibit at the Jamestown exposition. (61)

OCT. 18. Salt River in flood rises above the uncompleted Roosevelt Dam submerging working equipment. (61)

DEC. 1. *Bisbee Miner* reports that 500 Bisbee stockholders will share $525,000 as result of decision against South Bisbee Copper Co. (65)

DEC. 8. Record of real estate transactions show panic has done little to stop growth of Phoenix. (61)

Total major metals production in Arizona, $29,816,840. (22)

Total number of cattle in Arizona, 950,000; value, $15,663,000. (50)

1905 JAN. 2. Tucson City Council drives gambling houses out with high licenses. (74)

JAN. 8. Secretary of the Interior calls for bids on construction of irrigation works at Yuma. (70)

JAN. 10. Dick Wick Hall reports to land office in Prescott that he has established the settlement of Salome (Where She Danced) on the desert, seven miles from Harrisburg. (70)

JAN. 12. Territorial Teachers' Association in Flagstaff meeting files protest against joint statehood with New Mexico. (70)

JAN. 14. On eve of legislative session Phoenix is isolated by floods. (74)

JAN. 15. Report of Arizona Rangers to governor shows 1,058 arrests in two years. (74)

JAN. 16. Governor Brodie meets Legislature which denounces bill before Congress that would make Arizona and New Mexico one state. Brodie reports valuation of the Territory is $45,069,545 and that the indebtedness of Territory and counties is $3,055,274. (31)

FEB. 10. Joseph M. Kibbey, formerly member of Territorial supreme court is appointed Governor of Arizona by President Roosevelt. (74)

FEB. 11. The rains which are so copious are doing double duty in Arizona, insuring good crops, and at the same time keeping many of the legislators at home, thus preventing them from doing much damage in law making. (60)

FEB. 18. Governor Brodie returns to U. S. Army as a major. (31)

MAR. 26. Twenty-four Chinese who are smuggled over the Arizona-Mexico border in a boxcar are caught in Yuma. (74)

APRIL 2. Gas explosion in United Verde mine kills five and injures seven miners. (70)

APRIL 5. Judge R. E. Sloan enjoins miners from picketing German-American mine at Vivian. (70)

APRIL 13. Arizona Dam on Salt River near Phoenix goes out. (70)

MAY 13. Greer and St. Johns dams give way and St. Johns' Valley suffers heavy damage. (70)

MAY 26. Tucsonan stops runaway team on Stone Avenue by lassoing the horses. (74)

MAY 28. Republican and Democratic parties join in organizing Anti Joint-Statehood League and denounce consolidation with New Mexico under any conditions. (74)

JULY 1. L. C. Hughes, editor of the *Arizona Daily Star* and former governor of Arizona is arrested on a charge of criminal contempt of court. Found guilty he is fined $200. (74)

JULY. 12. Congressional delegation arrives in Tucson and tours Territory studying its claims to statehood. (74)

JULY 13. Office of U. S. Marshal is moved from Phoenix to Tucson. (74)

JULY 19. Yavapai County board of supervisors asks 300 taxpayers to explain why their assessments should not be raised. (74)

JULY 27. Department of the Interior orders consolidated land office moved from Tucson to Phoenix. (74)

AUG. 2. Unknown assassins fire into group of Silver Bell miners, killing two and wounding one. No known reason. (74)

SEPT. 5. Tucson passes ordinance requiring owners to register their automobiles and display number of same. (74)

SEPT. 5. Cloudburst in Granite Mountains sweeps away cattle, sheep and chickens in Williamson and Skull Valley. (70)

SEPT. 28. Legal wrangle over refusal of supervisors in Yavapai, Graham, and Mohave counties to increase assessment of the mines, as ordered by Territorial Board of Equalization, results in quashing of mandamus on a technicality. (70)

OCT. 4. Board of Supervisors of Maricopa County threatens to tear up the rails if Phoenix Street Railway Co., lays tracks on Grand Avenue in Phoenix. (70)

NOV. 10. Public schools in Tucson are reported to be so crowded that two pupils are occupying one seat. (74)

NOV. 14. José Lewis, Papago medicine man, is tried in district court for killing member of tribe. Lewis's defense is that Great Spirit told him the victim was a witch. Sentenced to 14 years at Yuma. (74)

NOV. 24. Arizona Bankers' Association denounces joint statehood. (74)

NOV. 28. Floods do great damage at San Carlos, Florence, Maricopa, Phoenix, Globe, and Dudleyville. Bridges on branch railroads are washed out. (74)

DEC. 5. Arizona seethes with indignation when President Roosevelt's message to Congress recommends joint statehood for Arizona and New Mexico. Towns hold mass meetings to protest. (74)

DEC. 11. Floods destroy sections of dam designed to stop Colorado River's flow into the Imperial Canal. (74)

DEC. 19. City Council of Tucson denounces jointure. Mass meeting of citizens does the same. (74)

DEC. 25. First Arizona State Fair opens in Phoenix under authority of a legislative act. (39)

DEC. 30. Tucson merchants announce that the closing of gambling houses has increased retail trade. (74)

DEC. 31. Five thousand citizens denounce joint statehood at State Fair in Phoenix. (74)

School census reports 15,241 children of school age are not attending school. Grade and high school pupils total 14,049, studying under 542 teachers. (13)

Total major metals production in Arizona, $40,246,861. (22)

Total number of cattle in Arizona, 100,000; value, $16,401,000. (50)

1906 JAN. 7. Five hundred Tucson citizens petition council to enforce ordinance forbidding spitting on sidewalks. (74)

JAN. 25. Public schools in Flagstaff are closed hastily as earthquakes rock city. (74)

JAN. 29. Western Union opens first direct wire between Tucson and Bisbee. (74)

MAR. 9. U. S. Senate kills House bill providing for joint statehood by passing Foraker amendment permitting Arizona to vote on jointure. (74)

APRIL. Arizona rushes carloads of cattle, refrigerated meats and dairy products to survivors of San Francisco earthquake and fire. (60–74)

MAY 2. Grand Jury scores management of Territorial Asylum for maltreatment of inmates. (70)

JUNE 7. First Arizona Bar Association is formed and incorporated, but dies from lack of interest. (9)

JUNE 1. Mule-drawn streetcar makes last trip in Tucson and first electric car travels to gate of The University of Arizona. (74)

JUNE 29. District court grants first Indian divorce to a Papago in Pima County. (74)

JULY 23. Troublesome Yaquis in Sonora trade for rifles in Arizona. Governor Kibbey issues proclamation forbidding such sales. (74)

AUG. 4. Democratic and Republican State Central Committees hold joint meeting in Phoenix and denounce statehood with New Mexico. (74)

AUG. 14. District clerks of Arizona receive copies of new naturalization regulations requiring aliens seeking citizenship to read, write, and speak English. (70)

SEPT. 20. President Roosevelt warns Governor Kibbey that joint statehood faction must have fair deal at the polls in coming election. (74)

OCT. 6. Fire destroys roundhouse and car shops of the Gila Valley, Globe, and Northern railroad. (74)

NOV. 6. Arizona votes overwhelmingly against jointure. Beats statehood with New Mexico 16,265 to 3,141. (56–74)

NOV. 8. Student prank at U. of A. ends in explosion of field gun and panic in women's dormitory. (74)

NOV. 10. Apache-Mohave brave kills three tribesmen and four squaws. Eludes three posses for four days. Surrenders at Jerome. (70)

NOV. 20. Phoenix votes out public gambling. (74)

DEC. 5. Worst of five floods suffered in three years practically wipes out Clifton. Business buildings and homes collapse or are swept away. Dead estimated at 15. Damage reaches $500,000. (74)

DEC. 8. Petrified Forest is made a National Monument. (33)

DEC. 18. Pushed by President Roosevelt, the Southern Pacific begins task of repairing new break in Colorado River which is pouring flood into Imperial Valley. (68)

Total major metals production in Arizona, $56,812,365. (22)

Total number of cattle in Arizona, 105,000; value, 18,356,000. (50)

1907 JAN. 11. City of Globe incorporated. (Letter)

JAN. 16. Sonoita Valley reports destructive floods which do great damage to fine ranches. (74)

JAN. 17. Santa Cruz river runs full to the bank and races through Tucson at eight miles an hour. (74)

JAN. 21. Twenty-fourth Territorial Legislature engages in bitter battle with Gov. Joseph H. Kibbey who insists on heavy taxation of mines, finally writes act which is a compromise; votes to move penitentiary to Florence and passes act to prevent women loitering in saloons. Public gambling is outlawed. (31)

FEB. 11. Second break in banks of Colorado is finally closed by work force of 1,000 men. (74)

FEB. 20. Tucson justice court holds that cattlemen and miners may wear guns lawfully for two hours after arrival in town. (74)

FEB. 25. University of Arizona Experiment Station announces plans for extensive trial plantings of sorghum on its Yuma farm. (74)

FEB. 28. Lieut. Harry Wheeler, Arizona Ranger, prevents double murder and although twice wounded, kills assailant on the main street of Benson. (74)

MAR. 22. Legislature moves Territorial prison from Yuma to Florence. (74)

APRIL 1. District attorney rules in Tucson that poker is illegal only if played publicly. (74)

APRIL 10. Western Federation of Miners attempts to organize and strike mines at Bisbee without success. (74)

JUNE 29. Fire destroys 80 buildings in Mexican section of Bisbee. Six hundred made homeless. (74)

AUG. 15. Entire Yuma contingent and group of Phoenix guardsmen ask to be mustered out of Territorial militia. Their complaints are that food was bad at the annual encampment and the officers too harsh. (74)

AUG. 16. Four men boiled in steam and one dies as boiler explodes in Southern Pacific roundhouse at Tucson. (74)

AUG. 17. Territorial Board of Equalization revalues mines, banks, cattle and all property and sets taxable wealth of Arizona at $77,372,156. (74)

AUG. 30. President Roosevelt announces administration will agree to separate statehood for Arizona and New Mexico. (74)

SEPT. 5. Smuggling of Chinese across Arizona border increases. U. S. Marshal captures 36 aliens and deports them. (74)

SEPT. 10. City Council passes an ordinance forbidding tuberculosis patients or other health seekers from erecting tents within city limits. Result: a city of tents springs up outside Tucson. (74)

OCT. 3. Yuma police stop poker games in saloons. Bisbee, Globe, and other towns consider taking same stand. (74)

OCT. 1. Arizona is feeling effect of financial panic and bank failures in New York. Mines close or curtail operations. Wages drop and workers are paid in clearing house scrip. (74)

OCT. 16. A departmental order sets apart lands for the Kaibab Paiute Reservation. (72)

OCT. 23. Solomon reports six murders in Graham County in one month. (74)

NOV. 1. Three Tucson firms are indicted by grand jury and charged with conspiracy to raise price of school books and supplies. (74)

NOV. 2. Knife-wielding robber holds up guests in four Prescott hotels in one night. One victim dies. (61)

DEC. 3. Pima County loses long fight to avoid paying interest and principal on the $150,000 in bonds which it gave promoters who promised a narrow gauge railroad to Globe, laid 10 miles of track, ran one train and dropped project. Supreme Court of the United States makes the final ruling. Cost to the county $320,000. (74)

DEC. 6. Valley Bank of Phoenix acquires the Home Savings Bank and Trust Co.

DEC. 17. President Theodore Roosevelt establishes the Tonto National Monument. (33)

DEC. 29. Deputy Sheriff White of Cochise County runs amuck in a sleeping car between Yuma and Gila Bend, terrifies women, tries to shoot conductor, and is finally manacled with his own handcuffs. (74)

DEC. 31. Phoenix and Tucson boards of trade issue cheerful resume of the year and state, "panic did little harm." (74)

Total major metals production in Arizona, $55,511,560. (22)

Total number of cattle in Arizona, 105,000; value, $18,448,000. (50)

1908 JAN. 11. First Grand Canyon National Monument is established. (33)

JAN. 9. Era of the all-night saloons ends in Tucson as council orders them closed at midnight. (74)

JAN. 21. Southern Pacific again pays employees in cash. Clearing house scrip used during panic disappears in Arizona. (74)

JAN. 24. Gifford Pinchot, chief U. S. forester, grants northern Arizona sheepmen permission to graze their flocks in the Prescott Forest Reserve for 60 days. (74)

FEB. 3. Phoenix saloon keepers counter ordinance which closes their bars at midnight and all day Sunday, by raising price of beer to ten cents a glass. Same action taken in Tucson previous year. (74)

FEB. 4. Interstate Commerce Commission practically quadruples freight rates on fuel oil between Bakersfield and Tucson. Latter city faces fuel famine. (61)

FEB. 13. Alarmed by number of smallpox cases Bisbee Board of Health orders all school children vaccinated. (74)

FEB. 20. Knights of Columbus meet in Tucson and form Territorial organization. (74)

FEB. 28. U. S. general land office ends long lawsuit by granting townsite in Oracle. (74)

MAR. 3. Town of Florence is incorporated. (Letter)

MAR. 9. Three carloads of giant Prescott pumps reach Tombstone for installation at the 1,000 foot level. (74)

MAR. 10. Prescott asks Gov. Kibbey for permission to form a company of national guardsmen. (74)

MAR. 11. Pima County is told that government will reimburse it for costs incurred by trials of criminal cases in which defendants are wards of the government. Expenses include cost of posse or Rangers. (74)

MAR. 12. Cold storage warehouse burns in Phoenix. Loss is $50,000. (61)

MAR. 22. Two men die and two are stabbed in gun and knife duel in Helvetia restaurant. Cause of trouble unknown. (74)

MAR. 26. University Experiment Station reports that five years of experiments with cotton at Yuma prove fine quality can be grown commercially. (74)

MAY 26. Eleven students in the preparatory school of the University at Tucson are caught playing "penny ante" in South Hall and are barred from dormitory. (74)

JUNE 8. Famous Baca Float No. 3, private land claim case, is finally resolved by the Secretary of the Interior and claims of settlers are declared valid. Immense grant includes rich mining districts in the Santa Rita Mountains. (74)

JUNE 13. Two thousand residents of Salt River Valley see Governor Kibbey pull lever which raises the gates in the newly completed Granite Reef dam. (61)

JULY 14. Bisbee High School Alumni launches first scholarship assistance movement in Arizona. (74)

JULY 21. Bartender who kills deputy sheriff in Williams escapes lynching when sheriff shoves him into the caboose as freight train pulls out for Flagstaff. (74)

AUG. 4. Disastrous rainstorm sends flood roaring down Tombstone Canyon in Bisbee. Library, postoffice, and merchants' basements are flooded. (74)

AUG. 5. Insane leper escapes confinement in Tombstone and frightens residents. (61)

AUG. 5. William Downing completes term of ten years in penitentiary for his part in the Stiles-Alvord holdup of Southern Pacific train, later resists arrest in Willcox and is killed by an Arizona ranger. (61)

AUG. 14. Tucson hangs its second murderer within a month. (61)

AUG. 23. Tempe has its first experience with a dry Sunday when new ordinance goes into effect. (61)

OCT. 14. Fire which blazes beyond control, rages in Bisbee business and residential section. Loss estimated at $500,000. (74)

NOV. 3. Mark Smith, veteran Arizona congressional delegate is unseated by Ralph Cameron, a Republican. (61)

NOV. 7. *Arizona Republic* stages first overland auto race in state. Four cars leave Los Angeles at midnight. Winner reaches Phoenix in 41½ hours. (61)

DEC. 31. Phelps Dodge Corp., names Dr. James Douglas as president. (44)

DEC. 31. Deposits in Arizona banks total $13,849,214. (12)

Total major metals production in Arizona, $41,811,975. (22)

Total number of cattle in Arizona, 102,500; value, $20,099,000. (50)

Town of Florence, Pinal County, incorporates. (32)

1909 JAN. 2. U. S. Dept. of Agriculture reports Arizona farm products totaled $9,304,000 in 1908. (74)

JAN. 18. Governor Kibbey meets with twenty-fifth and last Territorial Legislature which passes primary election law, repeals law creating Arizona Rangers, passes bill requiring that all voters must be able to read and write, and creates Greenlee County out of eastern section of Graham County. (31)

JAN. 28. Legislature threatens to discontinue Normal School at Flagstaff and abandon the building because of light registration. (74)

JAN. 29. Company of national guardsmen formed in Tucson. (74)

FEB. 5. School board in Prescott announces it is about to take determined steps to "stamp out the smoking habit" among students. (74)

FEB. 17. Geronimo, ruthless Apache enemy of Arizona, dies in captivity at Fort Sill. (39)

MAR. 15. Dick Wick Hall, flamboyant entrepreneur of Salome, Ariz., (Where She Danced) sets all Phoenix ablaze with samples of gold ore which he claims come from his desert bonanza. Railroad uses full page advertisements of special rates to Salome. Prospectors rush for the desert. Bonanza plays out. (61)

MAR. 20. Secretary of Interior orders Territorial officials — Arizona included — to stop spending time lobbying for bills in Washington. (74)

MAR. 30. Laguna diversion dam on the Colorado (Yuma Project) is completed. (74)

APRIL 1. Tucson police order motorists to observe municipal speed law of seven miles an hour. (74)

APRIL 24. Wickenburg is incorporated by vote of 36 to 5. (61)

MAY 1. Sheriff jails IWW miners who parade under a red flag in Globe. (61)

MAY 6. Richard E. Sloan, Arizona supreme court justice, becomes last Territorial Governor. (74)

MAY 26. Court dismisses twenty-two-year-old murder indictment against Geronimo. (74)

MAY 28. Two bankers who wrecked First National Bank in Bisbee get minimum sentences of five years. (74)

JUNE 4. Land-hungry citizens file on 25,000 acres of Agua Fria land through Phoenix land office. (61)

JUNE 6. First arrest for speeding recorded in Tucson when Steinfeld's chauffeur exceeds limit. (60)

JUNE 11. Miners in Yuma district stop work when thermometer reaches 110. (74)

JUNE 17. Portion of Gila Bend Indian Reservation reverts to public domain by executive order. (32)

JUNE 28. Masked man holds up crew of streetcar at the gates of the University. (74)

JULY 16. Army officers feud over who captured Geronimo. (74)

JULY 17. Twister lifts roof off Hotel Heidel in Tucson and drops a portion of it a block away. (74)

JULY 23. Armies of grasshoppers strip alfalfa fields of Mesa. (74)

JULY 26. Mayor of Tucson leads raid on gambling den in Chinese quarter and captures 26 men. (74)

JULY 30. Arizona leads world in production of copper ore from Jan. 1 to June 30. Phelps Dodge reported to have paid $2,224,730 in dividends during same period. (74)

AUG. 13. Discharged printer kills two linotype operators at *Bisbee Review* over labor troubles. (74)

OCT. 10. Constitutional Convention meets in Phoenix. (1)

OCT. 13. President Taft visits Arizona on transcontinental tour, speaks at Yuma, Tempe and Phoenix. Promises to do his best to bring statehood to Arizona. (74)

NOV. 11. Arizona and New Mexico white men steal so many horses from Navajo reservation that agency superintendents design a new tribal brand. (74)

NOV. 27. News columns show anti-gambling laws are widely ignored. Yavapai supervisor and Prescott councilman are caught and convicted. (74)

DEC. 19. Two trainmen killed and forty passengers injured when Southern Pacific jumps tracks near Benson. (74)

DEC. 25. Mexican Rurales fight desperate battle with six horsethieves who have been scourge of Arizona border. Kill four, wound two. (74)

Property valuation of Arizona declared to be $82,684,062. (39)

Deposits in Arizona banks total $17,715,326. (12)

Total major metals production in Arizona, $44,053,023. (22)

Total number of cattle in Arizona, 995,000; value, $19,820,000. (50)

Town of Wickenburg, Maricopa County, incorporates. (34)

1910 JAN. 2. Supai village in Cataract Canyon swept away by flood. Number of dead uncertain. (74)

JAN. 3. Clergymen, undertakers and cemeteries refuse to conduct Sunday funerals in Phoenix. (61)

FEB. 6. Mesa closes schools, churches, theaters, and all public meetings because of threatened epidemics of scarlet fever and diphtheria. (61)

FEB. 6. Dynamite blast at Ray kills seven men. (61)

MAR. 14. Tucson Women's Club tells mayor and council that grocery stores, butcher shops, and fruit stores are dirty and a menace to public health. (74)

MAR. 23. Nogales business district suffers loss of $50,000 in fire. (74)

APRIL 5. Territorial board of control accepts bids and orders construction of Pioneer's Home in Prescott. (61)

APRIL 10. Eastern interests get government concession for a dam in Sabino Canyon. Hope to sell water to Tucson. Concession later withdrawn. (74)

APRIL 25. Mesa Canal Co., sells holdings to government. (61)

MAY 5. Tucson stages giant celebration over opening of Tucson-West Coast of Mexico railway on Cinco de Mayo Day. (74)

MAY 12. Two boy bandits rob Maricopa and Phoenix train near Gila crossing, escape on horses but are rounded up when sheriff pursues them in an automobile. (61)

MAY 14. One thousand lots sold in Parker townsite in one day. (61)

MAY 26. Pima County Board of Supervisors rules that saloons will not be licensed in mining camps which have no police force. (74)

MAY 17. Hotel Adams in Phoenix is destroyed by fire. Loss is $200,000. (74)

JUNE 8. U. S. Department of Justice makes test case of law forbidding importation of unregistered Mexican labor and wins suit. (61)

JUNE 11. Board of Equalization sets value of taxable property of railroads at $20,125,515. (61)

JUNE 20. The Sixty-first Congress in enacting the act authorizing Arizona to establish state government grants 553,920 acres to the University. (5)

JUNE 20. President Taft signs enabling act for statehood. Arizona celebrates wildly. (74)

JULY 10. Independent labor party is organized in Arizona. (61)

JULY 11. Credentials committee of constitutional convention votes to bar Socialist delegates. (74)

JULY 13. Department of Interior approves plan to add system of Tempe Irrigation Canal Co., to the Salt River Project. Involves 17,000 acres. (61)

JULY 29. Gila County delegates to Constitutional Convention are first to pledge support to initiative, referendum and recall measures. (74)

SEPT. 12. Arizona elects delegates to the Constitutional Convention. Democrats in control, 36 to 16. (31–56)

OCT. 1. Interstate Commerce Commission orders reduction in freight rates for Arizona. (74)

OCT. 10. Constitutional Convention convenes in Phoenix, and George W. P. Hunt is elected chairman. Struggle ensues over inclusion of initiative, referendum and recall. All three are carried despite word from President Taft that he will veto constitution if it provides for recall of judges. (31–56)

OCT. 18. Mesa permitted to withdraw from Water Users Association, setting a precedent for Phoenix and Glendale. (61)

OCT. 20. Executive order No. 1256 adds lands to the Salt River Reservation. (32)

OCT. 28. Theological seminary for Indians contemplated south of Tucson. (74)

DEC. 1. Executive order No. 1267 enlarges the Fort Mohave Reservation. (32)

DEC. 31. Deposits in Arizona banks total $19,015,013. (12)

Average daily attendance in elementary schools, 19,144. High school daily attendance, 950. (13)

Total major metals production in Arizona, $42,731,519. (22)

Government reports show Arizona has 9,227 farms with 350,000 acres of improved land. Value of all farm property $29,993,847.

Total number of cattle, 950,000; value, $20,232,000. (49–50)

U. S. Census reports Arizona population as 204,354, a gain of 66.2 per cent in 10 years. (49)

City of Glendale, Maricopa County, incorporates. (34)

1911 JAN. 1. Underground water and low price of silver put an end to mining at Tombstone. (78)

JAN. 16. Home Missions of Congregational Church aid in organizing Church of Christ at Pearce. Douglas Graphic. (B)

JAN. 22. City marshal of Tucson announces all bicycle riders must ring bell when approaching an intersection. Penalty for failure can be fine of $50 or 50 days in jail. (60)

JAN. 31. Twenty-four leading citizens of Phoenix and 12 prominent men in Tucson issue public statement denying that the proposed state constitution is work of the Democratic party. (61)

FEB. 2. Executive order No. 1296 revokes executive order No. 1267 of December 1, 1910, and adds other lands to the Fort Mohave Reservation. (32)

FEB. 7. Ralph H. Cameron, Arizona's congressional delegate, warns that if people adopt proposed constitution, statehood will be defeated. (60)

FEB. 8. Two Mexicans guide four Chinese across boarder, kill three, wound one, rob the bodies and escape. (67)

FEB. 9. Proposed Arizona constitution carrying proposal for recall of judges is submitted to voters and passes 12,187 to 3,302. Thirteen out of 14 counties favor it. (31)

FEB. 9. M. P. Freeman, member of the Board of Regents, offers to bet $1,000 that Congress will accept constitution as written. (60)

FEB. 25. Matthew O. Roberts, twenty-two-year-old Papago, is first Indian to take a civil service technical examination. (60)

MAR. 18. Theodore Roosevelt dedicates dam bearing his name and sets machinery in motion which opens three gates. (61)

MAR. 22. Executive order No. 1322 makes the Salt River Reservation available to such Indians as the Secretary of the Interior may wish. (32)

APRIL 15. President William Howard Taft announces he will veto joint resolution of Congress providing statehood for Arizona because of proposed constitution including recall of judges. (56)

APRIL 18. Mexican rebels and Federals battle in streets of Agua Prieta, and bullets rain on city of Douglas where four citizens are wounded. (61)

APRIL 18. Phoenix votes wet but Maricopa County votes dry. (61)

MAY 4. Cochise supervisors, angered because proposed State highway will bypass Bisbee, threaten campaign to move capitol from Phoenix to Tucson. (60)

JUNE 2. Henry F. Ashurst, candidate for Democratic nomination as U. S. Senator meets M. G. Burns, political opponent, in Prescott, and fist fight follows. Ashurst wins the fight and later the senatorial seat. (60)

JUNE 2. Executive Order No. 1368 reserves additional lands for the Hualapai Indians. (32)

JULY 1. Co. H, national guard in Yuma, elects a Mexican to rank of lieutenant. Adjutant general refuses to issue commission. (60)

JULY 4. Five hundred Tucson citizens sign petition asking council to move red light district known as "Gay Alley" from downtown to outskirts of the city. (60)

JULY 8. City of Prescott presents University of Arizona with handsome iron gates. (60)

JULY 12. President Taft announces that he will veto Arizona constitution if it provides for recall of judges. (61)

JULY 30. Globe has so many fires that insurance companies refuse to write further policies. (61)

JULY 31. Executive Order No. 1387 adds certain lands to the Gila River Reservation. (32)

AUG. 8. U. S. Senate passes resolution granting statehood to both New Mexico and Arizona. (60)

AUG. 9. House concurs in Senate statehood resolution. (60)

AUG. 14. President Taft vetoes resolution giving statehood to Arizona and writes strong message explaining his action. (60)

AUG. 19. Congress passes new joint statehood resolution, eliminating recall of judges. (56)

AUG. 21. President Taft signs the amended statehood bill at 3:09 p.m., and says, "Gentlemen, it is done." (60)

AUG. 30. Henry F. Ashurst has a second tiff, this time in Prescott store with Michael Conniff. Friends break it up. (60)

AUG. 31. Railroads cut passenger fares to Arizona anticipating rush of settlers. Fare from Chicago to Tucson is $35. (60)

SEPT. 6. Fire destroys one wing of State Asylum in Phoenix. Militia called out to guard 160 patients who are evacuated safely. (60)

SEPT. 6. Inspector of weights and measures finds 30 out of 33 scales in Tucson give short weight. (60)

SEPT. 11. Phoenix breaks ground for handsome new polytechnic high school building. (60)

SEPT. 11. Free liquor passed out at Republican campaign headquarters on Meyer Street results in two shootings. (60)

SEPT. 28. Executive order adds lands to the Salt River Reservation. (32)

OCT. 23. Executive order adds certain lands to the Gila River Reservation. It also amends the executive order of June 14, 1879, pertaining to the Salt River Reservation. (32)

NOV. 7. Automobiles and roads are improving. Road race from Los Angeles to Phoenix sets new record of 20 hours, 22 minutes. (60)

DEC. 12. First state election is held in Arizona. George W. P. Hunt is elected governor, Sidney P. Osborn, secretary of state, Henry F. Ashurst, and Marcus A. Smith are the first U. S. Senators and Carl Hayden becomes the first congressman. (56)

DEC. 31. Report of Territorial Auditor shows the combined resources of Arizona banks to be $27,094,316. (68)

Total major metals production in Arizona, $44,157,223. (22)

Total number of cattle in Arizona, 915,000; value, $22,123,000. (50)

1912 JAN. 2. Weather Bureau reports that December was coldest month in Phoenix history. Mercury dropped below freezing on 18 days. (68)

JAN. 12. Running gun battle in Phoenix ends in capture of last of gang of outlaws who had terrified the city for weeks. (68)

JAN. 15. First annual auto show in Arizona opens in Phoenix. (68)

FEB. 13. Governor Sloan marks last day of administration by pardoning eight convicts serving life sentences for murder. (68)

FEB. 14. President Taft signs necessary proclamation making Arizona a state. George W. P. Hunt is inaugurated as governor and entire state celebrates wildly. (68)

FEB. 20. *Glendale News* established. (11)

MAR. 1. First session of the state legislature convenes and writes imposing list of laws including the following; child labor law making 14 years the minimum age, employers liability law, ratification of proposed Constitutional amendment enabling Congress to tax incomes, establishment of county drainage districts, free textbooks for common schools, establishment of a uniform public school system and its maintenance, creation of State Horticultural Commission, State Tax Commission, wider powers for Corporation Commission, new military code and reorganization of national guard. Other accomplishments are support of the University's experiments in dry farming, and appropriation of $5,000 for education of the blind, deaf, and dumb. The legislature also petitions Congress to open the rich mineral lands of the Colorado Indian Reservation to private development.

MAY 17. Legislature sends joint resolution to Congress asking that boundaries of the Colorado Indian Reservation set in 1865 be changed so as to free certain rich mineral lands for private exploitations. (Session Laws of Arizona)

MAY 18. Act providing for organization of irrigation districts approved. Free textbooks for common schools provided by act of Legislature. Arizona provides for establishment and maintenance of general and uniform public school system. State horticultural commission established. Employers' Liability Law established.

MAY 21. *Chandler Arizonan* established. (52)

MAY. 24. Legislature provides for new military code and for organization and regulation of National Guard.

MAY 23. Special session of the state legislature passes acts providing for regulation of railroad fares, workingmen's compulsory compensation, taxes on gifts, legacies and inheritances, operation of motor vehicles, construction and maintenance of state highways and bridges and enforcement of pure food standards. (State Session Laws)

MAY 28. Executive order 1538 sets aside the Ak Chin (Maricopa) Reservation for the "Maricopa band of Papago Indians." It is today inhabited entirely by Papago and Pima Indians. (32)

MAY 29. Executive order reserves additional lands for the Hualapai Project. (1)

JUNE 29. First Colorado River water turned into Yuma Reclamation Project June 29. (1)

JUNE 30. First report on public schools in first year of statehood shows 33,310 students enrolled or 78 percent of school population. Average daily attendance 68 percent. Total number of teachers 877. Total number of grammar and primary schools 233. Total number of high schools 16. Six counties without high schools. (13)

NOV. 5. Arizona holds general election and returns recall of the judiciary to constitution. (56–61–74)

DEC. 31. Deposits in Arizona banks total $28,452,422. (12)

Total number of cattle in Arizona, 970,000; value, $29,217,000. (50)

Total major metals production in Arizona, $67,050,784. (22)

First commercial crop of 375 bales of Pima Cotton is grown in the Salt River Valley, Yuma and Imperial Valley by 75 farmers. (43)

BIBLIOGRAPHY

Letters in parentheses following certain entries indicate the location of materials in the following libraries: (A) University of Arizona Library, Special Collections Division; (B) Arizona Pioneers' Historical Society, Tucson; (C) Arizona State Department of Library and Archives, Phoenix.

1. Adams, Ward R. and Richard E. Sloan, *History of Arizona.* Phoenix: Record Publishing Co., 1930. 4 vols.
2. *Arizona and Its Heritage.* Tucson: University of Arizona, 1936. (University of Arizona, General Bulletin no. 3).
3. *Arizona and the West.* vol. 1– 1959–
4. *Arizoniana.* vol. 1– 1960–
5. Arizona. Board of Regents. Records on file in the office of the President of the University of Arizona.
6. Arizona Development Board. *Historical Markers in Arizona.* Phoenix, [1958?] 2 vols.
7. *Arizona Historical Review.* vol. 1–7, 1928–36.
8. *Arizona, Its People and Resources,* Edited by Jack L. Cross, Elizabeth Shaw and Kathleen Scheifele. Tucson: University of Arizona Press, 1960.
9. *Arizona Law Review.* vol 1– 1959–
10. *Arizona Medicine.* vol. 1– 1944–
11. *Arizona Publisher.* vol. 1– 1955–
12. *Arizona Statistical Review.* 1945–
13. Arizona. State Department of Education. *Report of the Superintendent of Public Instruction.* 1875– (A C)
14. Bartlett, John Russell. *Personal Narrative of Explorations and Incidents in Texas, New Mexico, California, Sonora and Chihuahua.* N. Y.: D. Appleton & Co., 1854. 2 vols.
15. Bents, Doris Winnifred. *The History of Tubac, 1752–1948.* Tucson, 1949. Unpublished Master's thesis, University of Arizona. (A)
16. Brandes, Ray. *Frontier Military Posts of Arizona.* Globe, Ariz.: Dale Stuart King, 1960.
17. Cleland, Robert Glass. *A History of Phelps Dodge, 1834–1950.* N.Y.: A. A. Knopf, 1952.
18. Corle, Edwin. *The Gila, River of the Southwest.* N.Y.: Rinehart & Co., 1951.
19. Cosulich, Bernice. *Tucson.* Tucson: Arizona Silhouettes, 1953.
20. Darton, Nelson Horatio. *A Résumé of Arizona Geology.* Tucson: University of Arizona, 1925. (Arizona State Bureau of Mines Bulletin no. 119).
21. Dunning, Charles H. and Edward H. Peplow Jr. *Rocks to Riches.* Phoenix: Southwest Publishing Co., 1959.
22. Elsing, Morris J. and Robert E. S. Heineman. *Arizona Metal Production.* Tucson: University of Arizona, 1936. (Arizona State Bureau of Mines Bulletin no. 140).
23. Farish, Thomas Edwin. *History of Arizona.* Phoenix, 1915–18. 8 vols.
24. Forbes, Robert H. *Crabb's Filibustering Expedition into Sonora, 1857.* Tucson: Arizona Silhouettes, 1952.
25. Governor's (territorial) reports to the Secretary of the Interior. (A B C)
26. Granger, Byrd H. *Will C. Barnes' Arizona Place Names.* Revised and enlarged. Tucson: University of Arizona Press, 1960.
27. Greever, William S. *Arid Domain: the Santa Fe Railway and Its Western Land Grant.* Stanford, Calif.: Stanford University Press, 1954.
28. Hopkins, Ernest J. and Alfred Thomas Jr. *The Arizona State University Story.* Phoenix: Southwest Publishing Co., 1960.
29. Horton, Arthur C. *An Economic, Political and Social Survey of Phoenix and the Valley of the Sun.* Tempe: Southside Progress, 1941.
30. *The Howell Code.* Adopted by the First Legislative Assembly of Arizona. Prescott: Office of the Arizona Miner. 1865.
31. Kelly, George H. *Legislative History, Arizona, 1864–1912.* Phoenix: Manufacturing Stationers, 1926.
32. Kelly, William H. *Indians of the Southwest: a Survey of Indian Tribes and Indian Administration in Arizona.* Tucson: University of Arizona Bureau of Ethnic Research, 1953.
33. King, Dale S. editor. *Arizona's National Monuments.* Santa Fe, N. M.: Southwestern Monuments Association, 1945. (Popular Series no. 2).

34. League of Arizona Cities and Towns. *Directory of Arizona City and Town Officials.* 1953/54–
35. Luttrell, Estelle. *Newspapers and Periodicals of Arizona, 1859–1911.* Tucson; University of Arizona, 1950. (General Bulletin no. 15).
36. Martin, Douglas D. *The Lamp in the Desert: the Story of the University of Arizona.* Tucson: University of Arizona Press, 1960.
37. Martin, Douglas D. *Yuma Crossing.* Albuquerque: University of New Mexico Press, 1954.
38. Martin, Douglas D. *Tombstone's Epitaph.* Albuquerque: University of New Mexico Press, 1951.
39. McClintock, James H. *Arizona, Prehistoric, Aboriginal, Pioneer, Modern.* Chicago: S. J. Clarke, 1916. 3 vols.
40. McClintock, James H. *Mormon Settlement in Arizona: a Record of Peaceful Conquest in the Desert.* Phoenix, 1921.
41. McCrea, Samuel Pressly. *The Establishment of the Arizona School System.* [Stanford, Calif.] 1902. An unpublished thesis from Stanford University. (A)
42. Miller, Joseph. *The Arizona Story, Compiled and Edited from Original Newspaper Sources.* N.Y.: Hastings House, 1952.
43. McGowan, Joseph C. *History of Extra-Long Staple Cottons.* El Paso: Su Pima Association of America and Arizona Cotton Growers Association, 1961.
44. Peplow, Edward H. Jr. *History of Arizona.* N.Y.: Lewis Historical Publishing Co., 1958. 3 vols.
45. Powell, Donald M. *The Peralta Grant: James Addison Reavis and the Barony of Arizona.* Norman: University of Oklahoma Press, 1960.
46. Rand, Lenox H. and Edward B. Sturgis, editors. *The Mines Handbook.* vol. xviii. N.Y., Mines Information Bureau, 1931.
47. Salsbury, Cora B. *Forty Years in the Desert: a History of Ganado Mission, 1901–1940.* [Ganado, Ariz., 1940?]
48. U. S. Dept. of the Interior. *Report on the United States and Mexican Boundary Survey . . . by William H. Emory.* Washington: Cornelius Wendell, 1857. 2 vols. in 3. (34th Congress, 1st Session, House Executive Document no. 135).
49. U. S. Bureau of the Census, decennial census reports.
50. U. S. Agricultural Economics Bureau. *Livestock on Farms, Jan. 1, 1867–1919.* Washington, 1938.
51. U. S. War Dept. *Pacific Railroad Explorations and Surveys.* Washington, 1855–59. 11 vols. (33rd Congress, 2nd Session, Senate Executive Document no. 78).
52. U. S. War Dept. Letter to Douglas D. Martin.
53. Wagoner, J. J. *The History of the Cattle Industry in Southern Arizona, 1540–1940.* Tucson: University of Arizona, 1952. (Social Science Bulletin no. 20).
54. Weeks, Stephen B. *History of Public School Education in Arizona.* Washington: U. S. Bureau of Education, 1918. (Bulletin 1918, no. 17).
55. Woodward, Arthur. *Feud on the Colorado.* Los Angeles: Westernlore Press, 1955.
56. Wyllys, Rufus Kay. *Arizona, the History of a Frontier State.* Phoenix: Hobson & Herr, 1950.
57. Works Progress Administration. Historical Records Survey. *Inventory of the County Archives of Arizona.* Phoenix, 1938– Only Maricopa, Pima and Santa Cruz published.

NEWSPAPERS

58. *Alta California,* San Francisco. (A)
59. *Arizonian,* Tubac and Tucson. (B)
60. *Arizona Weekly and Daily Star,* Tucson. (A B)
61. *Arizona Republic,* Phoenix. (B C)
62. *Arizona Sentinel,* Yuma. (B C)
63. *Bisbee Daily Review.* (B)
64. *Florence Tribune.* (B C)
65. Bisbee *Miner.* (B C)
66. *Florence Tribune.* (B C)
67. Nogales *Oasis.* (A B)
68. *Phoenix Gazette.* (B C)
69. *Phoenix Herald.* (B C)
70. Prescott *Journal and Journal-Miner.* (B C)
71. *Prescott Weekly Courier.* (B C)
72. Phoenix, *Salt River Herald.* (B C)
73. *San Francisco Bulletin.* (B)
74. *Tucson Daily and Weekly Citizen.* (B C)
75. *Tempe News.* (B C)
76. Tucson, *Arizona Enterprise.* (B)
77. Yuma, *Arizona Sentinel.* (B C)
78. *Tombstone Epitaph.* (B)

INDEX

Adams, George H.: Oct. 12, 1879;
Mar. 6, 1881
Ajo: Aug. 4, 1854
Aldrich, Mark A.: Aug. 26, 1860
Algodones Grant: May 24, 1898;
Jan. 6, 1901
Allen, H. J.: Jan. 8, 1904
Allen, John B.: July 27, 1864
Almonds: Sept. 14, 1898
Alvord, Burt: Dec. 15, 1903;
Feb. 19, 1904
Apache County: Sept. 28, 1878
Apache Indians: *see also* Massacres;
Cochise; Geronimo; Feb. 4, 1861;
July 21, 1861; Apr. 15, 1862;
Oct. 31, 1865; Feb. 3, 1874;
Apr. 10, 1876; June 11, 1876;
Apr. 21, 1877; Sept. 16, 19, 1881;
Apr. 27, 1898; June 22, 1902
Apache Kid: Nov. 2, 1889;
July 3, 1893; Sept. 12, 1893
Apache Pass, battle at: July 15, 1862
Arivaca Ranch: Mar. 24, 1856
Arizona Bar Association:
June 17, 1906
Arizona Cattle Growers: Jan. 5, 1904
ARIZONA CITIZEN: Oct. 15, 1870
Arizona City: Jan. 6, 1873
Arizona Copper Co.: Aug. 4, 1854
Arizona County: Jan. 31, 1860
Arizona Dam: Apr. 13, 1905
Arizona Medical Association:
May 25, 1892
ARIZONA MINER: Mar. 8, 1864
Arizona Pioneers' Historical
Society: Jan. 31, 1884; Feb. 9, 1890;
Mar. 25, 1891; Oct. 14, 1897
Arizona Press Association:
Feb. 9, 1891
Arizona Rangers: Jan. 2, 1867;
Jan. 21, 1901; July 21, 1901;
Jan. 19, 1903; Jan. 15, 1905;
Feb. 28, 1907; Jan. 18, 1909
Arizona Rangers, petition for:
Feb. 25, 1859
ARIZONA REPUBLICAN:
Nov. 11, 1890
ARIZONA SENTINEL:
Mar. 10, 1872
ARIZONA SILVER BELT:
Sept. 28, 1878
ARIZONA STAR: Mar. 1, 1877
Arizona State Fair: Dec. 25, 1905
ARIZONIAN: Mar. 3, 1859;
Aug. 4, 1859

Army *see* U. S. Army
Army of the West: Oct. 20, 1846
Arthur, Chester A.: May 3, 1882
Atlantic and Pacific Railroad:
July 1, 1881
Ashurst, Henry F.: June 2, 1911;
Aug. 30, 1911; Dec. 12, 1911
Automobile races: Nov. 7, 1908;
Nov. 7, 1911
Automobiles: May 4, 1904;
Sept. 5, 1905; Apr. 1, 1909;
Jan. 15, 1912

Baca Float: June 8, 1908
Banks: Jan. 1879; Aug. 16, 1893;
Dec. 15, 1899; Nov. 13, 1903;
Jan. 14, 1904; Dec. 6, 1907;
May 28, 1909
Baptist church: Sept. 16, 1879
Barbers: May 16, 1898
Barnes, W. H.: Nov. 3, 1893
Bascom, George H.: Feb. 4, 1861
Baths open at Tucson: Sept. 23, 1879
Baylor, John R.: Aug. 1, 1861
Beale, Edward F.: Sept. 4, 1857
Bicycles: Jan. 22, 1911
Birch, James E.: June 22, 1857
Bisbee: Jan. 9, 1902
BISBEE DAILY REVIEW:
May 6, 1896
Bisbee Mines *see also* Phelps Dodge
Co.: Dec. 1, 1904
Blake, Charles M.: Dec. 28, 1866
Bloody Tanks: Feb. 23, 1864
Blythe, John L.: Oct. 15, 1873
Boston Party: July 4, 1876
Boundary Survey: Jan. 31, 1855
Bowers, Nathan: Nov. 10, 1871
Brodie, Alexander O.: May 7, 1902;
Feb. 18, 1905
Buchanan, James: Dec. 8, 1857
Buehman, H.: Jan. 5, 1898
Buck, George: Feb. 13, 1872
Burnett, James C.: July 3, 1897
Burns, M. G.: June 2, 1911
Burn, T. D.: Aug. 2, 1877
Butterfield Mail: Oct. 1, 1858;
Feb. 1, 1861

California Column: May 20, 1862
Callville: Dec. 17, 1864
Camels: May 16, 1855; Sept. 4, 1857
Cameron, Ralph: Nov. 3, 1908
Camp Bowie: July 15, 1862
Camp Calhoun: Oct. 2, 1849

La Paz: Jan. 1862; Jan. 30, 1876
Lawyers: May 7, 1872
Legislature:
first, Sept. 26, 1864
second, Dec. 6, 1865
third, Oct. 3, 1866
fourth, Sept. 4, 1867
fifth, Nov. 10, 1868
sixth, Jan. 11, 1871
seventh, Jan. 6, 1873
eighth, Jan. 6, 1875
ninth, Jan. 11, 1877
tenth, Jan. 6, 1879
eleventh, Jan. 3, 1881
twelfth, Jan. 8, 1883
thirteenth, Mar. 10, 1885
fourteenth, Mar. 10, 1887
fifteenth, Jan. 29, 1889
sixteenth, Jan. 19, 1891
seventeenth, Feb. 13, 1893
eighteenth, Jan. 21, 1895
nineteenth, Jan. 18, 1897
twentieth, Jan. 16, 1899
twenty-first, Jan. 21, 1901
twenty-second, Jan. 19, 1903
twenty-third, Jan. 16, 1905;
Feb. 11, 1905
twenty-fourth, Jan. 21, 1907
twenty-fifth, Jan. 18, 1908
first state, Mar. 1, 1911
Libel: Apr. 8, 1893
Library:
territorial, Mar. 14, 1866
Phoenix, Jan. 16, 1891
Tucson, Mar. 16, 1890
Lincoln, Dr. Able: Jan. 1850
Littlefield: Dec. 2, 1864
Lowell Observatory: May 22, 1894;
Mar. 31, 1895
Lynchings:
Bisbee, Sept. 11, 1882
Flagstaff, Jan. 19, 1887
Globe, Aug. 23, 1882
Holbrook, Apr. 24, 1885;
Aug. 15, 1888
Tucson, Mar. 24, 1872; Aug. 6, 1873

McAteer, P.: Dec. 1, 1873;
Dec. 1, 1883
McCord, Myron H.: May 19, 1897;
July 18, 1897; July 19, 1898
McCormick, Richard C.:
Mar. 9, 1864; Dec. 6, 1865;
Apr. 10, 1867; Oct. 15, 1870
McCracken, Jackson: Aug. 8, 1874

McKinley, William: May 8, 1900
McWillie, Marcus: Mar. 11, 1862
Machebeuf, Joseph P.: May 1, 1859
Mail see Postal Service
Mangas Coloradas: July 21, 1861
Mansfeld, J. S.: Nov. 27, 1886
Maricopa and Phoenix Railroad:
July 3, 1887
Maricopa County: Feb. 28, 1871
Maricopa County courthouse:
June 7, 1879
Maricopa reservation: May 28, 1912
Mason, John S.: Oct. 31, 1865
Masonic lodge: July 25, 1865;
Dec. 31, 1881
Massacres: Mar. 11, 1864; Oct. 9, 1869
Camp Grant, Apr. 10, 1871
ferrymen at Yuma, Apr. 23, 1850
Oatman family, Mar. 28, 1851
Mesa Canal Co.: Apr. 25, 1910
Mesquite: Mar. 18, 1898
Messea, Father Carlos: Dec. 7, 1864
Meteor: Feb. 24, 1897
Methodist church: Apr. 4, 1874;
Oct. 12, 1879; Mar. 6, 1881;
Oct. 3, 1903
Mexican band declared nuisance:
July 7, 1892
Mexican War declared:
May 13, 1846
Miles, Nelson A.: Aug. 25, 1886;
Nov. 8, 1887; Oct. 20, 1890
Militia: Apr. 14, 1870; Aug. 15, 1907
Milton, Jeff: Feb. 15, 1890
Mineral production see next to last
item each year
Mine assessments: Sept. 28, 1905
Mogollon Rim tunnel: Aug 18, 1883
Mohave County: May 5, 1867
Monterey Ditch Co. Jan. 7, 1871
Mormon Battalion: Dec. 17, 1846
Mormon missions: Mar. 23, 1876
Mormon academy, St. Johns:
Jan. 14, 1889
Mormon temple: Jan. 24, 1887
Mormons at Tubac: 1851
Mossman, Burton W.: July 21, 1901
Mowry, Sylvester: Dec. 8, 1857;
Sept. 3, 1858; July 3, 1859;
Aug. 4, 1859; 1860; June 6, 1862
Mowry Mine: 1860
Murders:
Bisbee, Aug. 13, 1909
Graham County, Oct. 23, 1907
Helvetia, Mar. 22, 1908